THE ULTIMATE MINNESOTA COOKIE BOOK

The Ultimate Minnesota Cookie Book

100 Best Recipes from the *Star Tribune*'s Holiday Cookie Contest

LEE SVITAK DEAN AND RICK NELSON

PHOTOGRAPHY BY TOM WALLACE

University of Minnesota Press

MINNEAPOLIS / LONDON

Lee Svitak Dean, Rick Nelson, and Tom Wallace were employees of Star Tribune Media Company LLC in Minneapolis, Minnesota. Some of the writing and photographs in this book were first published in the *Star Tribune* newspaper or on StarTribune.com. Copyright for those articles and photographs is to Star Tribune Media Company LLC; they are reprinted here with permission. Star Tribune retains all copyright and syndication rights for those articles and photographs.

Photographs on pages xiii–xiv by Rick Nelson
Photograph on page 220 by Lee Svitak Dean

Published by the University of Minnesota Press
111 Third Avenue South, Suite 290
Minneapolis, MN 55401-2520
http://www.upress.umn.edu

ISBN 978-1-5179-1817-0 (hc)

A Cataloging-in-Publication record for this book is available from the Library of Congress.

Printed in China on acid-free paper

The University of Minnesota is an equal-opportunity educator and employer.

30 29 28 27 26 25 24   10 9 8 7 6 5 4 3 2 1

In flour-dusted gratitude
for the many bakers who put the merry
into sweet treats

Contents

Introduction

EVERY COOKIE TELLS A STORY. THIS IS OURS.

IN 2003, Rick Nelson offered a simple suggestion that was to change our holiday planning for years to come in the Taste section of the *Star Tribune*: "Let's have a cookie contest."

Sounds simple enough: select the best cookie from a pile of entries. How difficult could that be?

Well, after amassing 102 winning recipes, culled from nearly 5,000 submissions over two decades, we can say that it was not only a lot of work—both in the office and in the kitchen—but the contest also became our own beloved holiday tradition, one that left an annual trail of flour dust, toasted almonds, and bits of chocolate along the way.

The delicious result from all that scrutiny—and all that baking—is in your hands: the best recipes from the first twenty years of the *Star Tribune* Holiday Cookie Contest. Our earlier compilation from the contest, *The Great Minnesota Cookie Book* (University of Minnesota Press, 2018) featured its first fifteen years of award winners.

This "Ultimate" look at the cookie contest includes every "Great" recipe from our first cookbook, along with twenty-five winners that came out of the competitions between 2018 and 2022. We've also added a few essays and some of our own favorite family recipes.

This compilation of the *Star Tribune* Holiday Cookie Contest winners is our way of inviting you into the kitchen. We can't think of a better place to gather as we close out our involvement with the contest's December tradition. Bakers, preheat your ovens!

When we staged that first contest in 2003, we never thought that it would evolve into an annual event that would capture the imaginations of Minnesota bakers. We certainly didn't foresee that it would introduce cookie recipes that would become cherished classics in countless households from Minneapolis to Moorhead.

The contest also quickly became a much-anticipated highlight on our calendars. How many people get to say that they had this much fun at work? We are fortunate, indeed.

The two decades of Minnesota-made ingenuity represented in these pages serve as a reminder that cookies have the power to change the world. Or, at least, to change the day for those lucky enough to find themselves near a homemade cookie. Who can be grumpy with an Almond Palmier, a Tiramisu Twist, or a Nut Goodie Thumbprint in hand?

All we are saying is, give cookies a chance.

Our annual event has sent many local bakers to the kitchen year-round to experiment and fine-tune their recipes, in hopes of winning the coveted designation for Minnesota's top cookie of the season. The contest inevitably resulted in sold-out specialty ingredients in local supermarkets. There was the run on almond flour one year, and on pistachios and sliced almonds during others, the reactions of frenzied bakers in search of the season's must-have item.

That popularity came as no surprise to us, given the baking culture of the state—all those cold days and nights to fill and, historically, a heritage with a fondness for baked goods (thank the Scandinavians and Germans). Not so incidentally, Minnesota is the home of some of the country's largest butter and flour producers, and Minnesota farmers harvest more sugar beets than any other state. The Mississippi River's St. Anthony Falls powered the grain mills. And we have a state muffin—blueberry! Let us not forget that the granddaddy of all baking contests, the Pillsbury Bake-Off, was born in Minneapolis.

So, yes, baking is in our DNA.

Our contest prep always began in mid-September as we posted the announcements for the competition. Over the next four weeks, entries trickled in, until days before the deadline when a barrage of recipes would suddenly appear. Readers aren't much different from reporters—we all need deadlines!

Minutes after the clock struck noon—always the cutoff time—we began to sift through the stack of recipes, some handwritten in the careful script of a veteran baker, most of them printed from a computer. The entries arrived from all sorts of kitchens: from teachers representing their classrooms, from bakers in their twenties or in their nineties, and, once, from an inmate at the county jail. Most participants offered the story behind their cookie, sharing poignant tales of the link between past and present that so often revolve around the dinner table.

Over the years, as we heard from thousands of Minnesota bakers, a small group of contestants created recipes that routinely landed in the finalists' and winners' circles: Michelle Clark, Cheryl Francke, Joan Hause, and Patrice Johnson each had two; Cynthia Baxter and Janet Heirigs each had three; Lance Swanson had four; and Joanne Holtmeier was our all-time champ, with six.

The annual judging process began, naturally, with the recipe. The stack of between 200 to 350 entries awaited as we tried to figure out, one by one, which would taste better than the next. For the first cut, based on our longtime experience of reading recipes, we simply used our eyes to gauge which cookies had the most appeal as we sorted them into piles of "must have," "possible," and "not a chance."

Sometimes they were heirloom recipes that had been in families for generations; occasionally the contenders were cherished favorites that had been tweaked by bakers.

Original cookies often found their way into the mix, developed by contestants who tapped into current food trends (think sea salt, espresso, and brown butter—and, yes, even kale). Though the recipes didn't need to be created specifically for our contest, we valued cookies that would be new to most bakers—"new" being relative, of course—because the contest's goal was always to provide compelling, unexpected recipes to *Star Tribune* readers.

Another requirement: the recipes that made it to the winners' circle had to delight and inspire both longtime bakers and those entering the kitchen for the first time.

Each year, the selected finalists had to represent not only a breadth of flavors and textures for the home baker (we couldn't present all chocolate or all sandwich cookies, for example), but also a variety in appearance, since the winning treats were published in early December, a time when bakers are prepping for festive cookie platters. We also kept in mind our ever-growing archive of past winners, because we wanted to avoid overlap.

Though reading a recipe was a solid start, our contest's format relied heavily on baking. After all, a cookie's taste, scent, texture, and appearance cannot be scrutinized via the written word.

For the first year, Rick baked all twenty-two semifinalist recipes and hauled them into the *Star Tribune* newsroom for a food staff taste-off, an exhausting task he vowed never

to repeat. After that, we enlisted a stable of reliable bakers to prepare the recipes.

For the next eleven years, that role was filled by *Star Tribune* colleagues, and we followed a simple rule: those who baked for us could join us for the judging process. This annual October ritual would often attract up to two dozen newsroom staffers, who would gather in the newspaper's largest conference room and passionately argue the deficiencies and merits of cookies. Lots of cookies. The greatest number of semifinalist recipes was thirty-four, with most years hovering between eighteen and twenty-four.

In 2015, we shifted to the skills of a pastry chef and her professional crew and quickly established a successful routine. Working in well-equipped culinary teaching facilities, first at the Art Institutes International Minnesota in downtown Minneapolis and then at Burnsville High School in Burnsville, the team would prepare cookie doughs on a Friday afternoon, then return the following morning for baking and decorating. A few hours later, a small judging panel—which included Taste staffers, prior contest winners, and other accomplished bakers—would convene to assess the expertly prepared entries.

By necessity, the first pandemic contest required a bit of improvisation. After a flurry of back-and-forth emails, our team of pastry chef professionals, assisted by Taste staffers, baked cookies in their home kitchens, then delivered the results to a centrally located facility, otherwise known as Rick's garage, where cars were replaced with tables and all of the building's doors and windows were wide open for maximum fresh-air circulation. The judging panel dropped in, one by one, to collect samples of each cookie. After returning home, we logged in and conducted the taste-a-thon via Zoom.

No matter the venue, we traditionally began each year's marathon with a warning, based on our years of judging food contests: "Pace yourself. You don't have to eat the entire cookie."

Milk and water were in ready supply as palate cleansers for the tasters who were challenged with eating more cookies in an hour than most would otherwise consume over the course of a month. During the contest's first two decades, our judges collectively sampled nearly five hundred semifinalist cookies. We won't even begin to consider the calorie count.

As the judges sat at the table, the trays of cookies, in all their grandeur, offered an initial thrill, a buffet of treats that shouted "special occasion." Then reality set in. We

We received nearly five thousand entries to our annual contest over twenty years.

each cautiously nibbled a corner of the first contender. "Too many ingredients," mumbled one judge. "What am I supposed to be tasting?" Murmurs of agreement sounded off around the table.

The next cookie made the rounds. "The chocolate is nice, but the texture is off," noted a critic. "This is way too savory for a cookie," said another. And on it went, one by one, as the rejects piled up on overflowing paper plates, until a cookie finally captured our attention.

"I love this lemon flavor," said a judge with a smile. "This is a keeper."

More assessment: Is the cookie too sweet or too difficult to make? Are the ingredients readily available? Is it too ordinary, or will it sparkle on a holiday platter? Has a similar cookie been a contender in the past? Is a bar really a cookie? (We think so.) These are some of the questions we asked ourselves as we sampled each entry.

A small group of semifinalist cookies made the leap to potential finalists, often by a single indicator: judges would take a second bite.

The task of determining the winner from a group of five finalists often required plenty of discussion, compromise, and banter among the judges.

We videotaped a session once, thinking it would be of interest to readers to see how one cookie was chosen over another. Then, as we later watched it and saw the judges deliver their commentary with brutal honesty and candor (they were there to pick a winner, after all), we recognized that, sometimes, it's better not to hear what others think of your recipe. The concept of "Minnesota Nice" prevailed, and the video never made it to the newspaper's website.

Our contest has inspired our personal cookie-baking practices and brought back memories of our own family favorites, old and new, which we offer in this second edition of what we have always called "the cookie book." That link to the past plays a big part in a cookie's story. For us, that means Ranger Cookies and Peanut Butter Blossoms, as well as Sandbakkels and Salted Peanut Cookies. After all, cookies are meant to be shared, and that goes for the memories they bring and the traditions they create.

A skeptic may wonder how many new cookie recipes there can be. After all, the building blocks tend to be the same basic four: flour, butter, sugar, and eggs.

But that's just the beginning, of course. It's the cinnamon and cardamom, the almond paste and coconut, citrus and, of course, chocolate (semisweet, bittersweet, or white) and nuts (pecan, walnut, pistachio, hazelnut, almond, cashew, peanut, and macadamia), in all their delightful variations, that transform the ordinary into the extraordinary bite of perfection.

In the end, perhaps there is nothing simple about the cookie. Nothing, that is, except for its goodness. But don't take our word for it. Head to the kitchen and give these winners a try.

Your cookie platter is waiting, and we have 113 recipes for you to bake.

A Baker's Dozen

TIPS FOR GREAT COOKIES

1 BUILD THE FOUNDATION Before beginning, read the recipe from start to finish, twice. This will eliminate any surprises in terms of ingredients, timing, and advance preparation.

2 SHOP WISELY Unless otherwise noted, the cookie recipes in this book call for large eggs, all-purpose flour, unsalted butter, and whole milk. For the best results, use real extracts and not artificial ones, and fresh spices. Buy the latter in the bulk section; you'll save money by purchasing only what you need.

3 CONDUCT A TEST For infrequent bakers, here's a test to make sure that the leaveners in the pantry are still effective. For baking powder, stir 2 teaspoons into ½ cup of hot water, then look for bubbles. For baking soda, dissolve ¼ teaspoon into 2 teaspoons of vinegar, then look for bubbles. If there's no reaction, it's time for fresh replacements.

4 EQUIP YOUR KITCHEN Use flat, shiny, and rimmed medium- to heavy-gauge aluminum baking sheets; we like the half-sheet trays from Minnesota-made Nordic Ware (nordicware.com), which are widely available. Skip the nonstick coating and instead use—and reuse—parchment paper, a baker's best friend.

5 MEASURE CAREFULLY Spoon flour and powdered sugar into the measuring cup (rather than use the measuring cup as a scoop), and level the ingredients with a straightedge, such as a knife. Press brown sugar firmly into a dry measuring cup. Use clear measuring cups for liquids.

6 CHECK THE TEMPERATURE Room-temperature butter and eggs are essential cookie building-blocks. Butter is at room temperature when a light touch leaves a slight indentation, about 30 to 45 minutes outside the refrigerator. Do not use a microwave oven to coax butter to room temperature. Eggs will come to room temperature after about 30 to 45 min-utes outside the refrigerator. To speed up the process, place them in a bowl and cover them with warm tap water for about 10 minutes.

7 MIX LIKE A PRO When preparing the dough, take a moment to stop the electric mixer, scrape the bottom and sides of the bowl with a spatula, then resume mixing; repeat as necessary. To add ingredients, turn off the mixer, place the ingredients in the bowl, then resume mixing.

8 SCOOP IT UP For drop cookies that are uniform in size and bake evenly, use a portion scoop to shape the dough. It's a game changer. A one-tablespoon scoop of dough makes a 1-inch ball of dough.

9 STAY IN SHAPE To keep refrigerator cookie logs from going flat, wrap the dough logs in plastic wrap or wax paper, place them on a level shelf in the refrigerator, and give the dough a quarter-turn every 15 minutes for the first hour of refrigeration. Or store them inside the cardboard dowel of a roll of paper towels that has been cut, lengthwise, and opened.

10 KNOW YOUR OVEN Preheat the oven for at least 20 minutes. For true accuracy, invest in an oven thermometer. Major retailers sell reliable models for less than ten dollars, an expenditure that will quickly pay for itself. Move the thermometer around the oven prior to baking to determine if hot spots exist. Place one baking sheet at a time in the oven, using the middle rack. Rotate the baking sheet halfway through the baking time.

11 FOLLOW THE CLOCK If the recipe includes a range of baking times, begin by setting the timer for the least amount of time. If the oven has a convection function, use it; cookies will bake more evenly, because a small fan is circulating heat around the oven. Cookies bake faster in a convection oven, so plan accordingly.

12 KEEP COOL Between batches, cool the baking sheets completely (heat can cause dough to spread) by alternating among several baking sheets, or by running hot ones under cold water.

13 STORE AND FREEZE WISELY Most cookies remain fresh for up to a week when stored in an airtight container at room temperature. Store different cookies in separate containers so their flavors don't mingle. Freeze cookies undecorated; when ready to serve, thaw and decorate.

CHAPTER ONE

Sandwich Cookies

Alfajores

When Graciela Cuadrado-Vielguth of Coon Rapids moved north to the United States from her native Uruguay, she carried a taste of home with her: Alfajores. This delicate, buttery cookie (pronounced al-fa-HOR-es) is traditional throughout South America, and she made them a staple of her Christmas baking. While Alfajores require a few more steps than your basic drop cookie, they're definitely worth the extra fuss. "When my kids say, 'Why don't you make Alfajores?' I tell them, 'Okay, I'll make them, but you have to put them together,'" said Cuadrado-Vielguth.

MAKES 1 TO 4 DOZEN COOKIES

½ cup flour, plus extra for rolling dough

1 ¼ cups cornstarch

1 teaspoon baking powder

½ cup (1 stick) unsalted butter, at room temperature

¾ cup granulated sugar

1 egg

1 egg yolk

Freshly grated zest from ½ lemon

1 (13.4-ounce) can *dulce de leche* (see Note)

1 ½ cups shredded coconut, preferably desiccated (dried) and unsweetened

NOTE This dough must be prepared in advance. The large amount of cornstarch is correct. *Dulce de leche* (also called *cajeta* and *manjar*) is a thick caramel made from sweetened condensed milk; it's in the international food aisles of many supermarkets.

In a medium bowl, whisk together the flour, cornstarch, and baking powder, and reserve. In the bowl of an electric mixer on medium-high speed, beat the butter until creamy, about 1 minute. Gradually add the granulated sugar and beat until light and fluffy, about 2 minutes. Add the egg and egg yolk and beat until thoroughly combined. Add the lemon zest and beat until thoroughly combined. Reduce the speed to low, add the flour mixture, and mix until just combined. Cover the bowl with plastic wrap and refrigerate for at least 2 hours.

When ready to bake, preheat the oven to 350°F and line the baking sheets with parchment paper.

On a lightly floured surface using a lightly floured rolling pin, roll the dough to ³⁄₁₆-inch thickness. Using a cookie cutter, cut the dough into rounds of desired size (between 1 and 2 inches) and place 2 inches apart on the prepared baking sheets. Repeat with the remaining dough, gathering up scraps, re-rolling, and cutting until all the dough is used. Bake 11 to 12 minutes, making sure the cookies do not brown. Remove the cookies from the oven and cool for 2 minutes before transferring them to a wire rack to cool completely. (The cookies may be stored up to a week in an airtight container before assembling.)

Spread ½ teaspoon *dulce de leche* (more for larger cookies) on the flat side of one cookie. Place the flat side of a second cookie against the *dulce de leche*, as if making a sandwich. Press gently, just until the *dulce de leche* is at the edge of the cookies. Spread a very thin layer of the *dulce de leche* onto the sandwich edge, and roll the edge in the shredded coconut. Repeat with the remaining cookies.

Almond Sandwiches

Patricia Sanford of Edina has lovely stories to tell. "This recipe came down from my great-grandmother to my grandmother, to my mother, to me," she said. Although she's always called them Almond Sandwiches, other relatives refer to these family gems as plain old sugar cookies. "That would never do. They are far more than a sugar cookie," she said. "They just about melt in your mouth." Sanford is carrying the family's baking traditions forward. "My granddaughter is living with me right now, so I'm teaching her all the basics," she said. "I love that part of being a grandmother. You're not just cooking; you're telling stories. Cookies have always been a wonderful vehicle for telling stories, don't you think?"

MAKES 2 DOZEN COOKIES

FOR COOKIES

1 cup (2 sticks) unsalted butter, at room
   temperature
1/3 cup heavy cream
2 cups flour, plus extra for rolling dough

FOR FILLING

4 tablespoons (1/2 stick) unsalted butter,
   at room temperature
3/4 cup powdered sugar
1 tablespoon heavy cream
1/2 teaspoon almond extract
Food coloring, optional

NOTE This dough must be prepared in advance.

TO PREPARE COOKIES: In the bowl of an electric mixer on medium-high speed, beat the butter until creamy, about 1 minute. Add the cream and beat until thoroughly combined. Reduce the speed to low, add the flour, and mix until just combined. Form the dough into a disk, wrap in plastic wrap, and refrigerate for at least 30 minutes.

When ready to bake, preheat the oven to 350°F and line the baking sheets with parchment paper.

On a lightly floured surface using a lightly floured rolling pin, roll the dough to 1/8-inch thickness. Using a 2-inch cookie cutter, cut the dough into desired shape (cutting out the center of half of the cookies if desired) and place 1 inch apart on the prepared baking sheets. Repeat with the remaining dough, gathering up scraps, re-rolling, and cutting until all the dough is used. Bake until the edges of the cookies are lightly browned, 15 to 20 minutes. Remove the cookies from the oven and cool for 2 minutes before transferring them to a wire rack to cool completely.

TO PREPARE FILLING: In the bowl of an electric mixer on medium-high speed, beat the butter until creamy, about 1 minute. Reduce the speed to medium-low and add the powdered sugar, cream, and almond extract, and mix until light and fluffy, about 2 minutes. Add the food coloring (optional), 1 drop at a time, and mix until thoroughly combined.

TO ASSEMBLE COOKIES: Spread a dollop of filling on the flat side of one cookie. Place the flat side of a second cookie (which has the extra cutout, if using) against the filling, as if making a sandwich. Press gently, just until the filling is at the edge of the cookies. Repeat with the remaining cookies.

Apple Pecan Stars

When Jana Freiband of Minneapolis moved into her house, she planted a pair of what turned out to be highly productive Haralson apple trees. She channels her backyard bounty into crisps, pies, and galettes. Oh, and apple butter, which became her recipe's key ingredient. She reached for her star-shaped cookie cutter for a reason. "There's something about Christmas and stars," she said. "I've always related Christmas to something brilliant in the sky, rather than the traditional trees or wreaths. I always decorate the front of my house with stars." The Haralson apple was developed by the University of Minnesota.

MAKES 1 1/2 DOZEN COOKIES

FOR COOKIES

2 cups flour, plus extra for rolling dough

1/2 teaspoon baking powder

2 tablespoons powdered sugar, plus more for decoration

1/8 teaspoon salt

2 teaspoons ground cinnamon

2 teaspoons ground cardamom

3/4 cup pecans, toasted (see Note)

1/2 cup (1 stick) unsalted butter, at room temperature

1/4 cup granulated sugar

1 egg

1 teaspoon vanilla extract

1/4 cup milk or water, as needed

FOR FILLING

4 apples, peeled and sliced

1/4 teaspoon ground cinnamon

1/4 teaspoon freshly grated nutmeg

1/4 teaspoon ground cardamom

Pinch of ground cloves

1/4 cup packed light brown sugar

1/2 teaspoon freshly squeezed lemon juice

NOTE This dough must be prepared in advance. For the filling, commercially prepared apple butter is readily available, if you prefer not to make your own. To toast pecans, place the nuts in a dry skillet over medium heat, and cook, stirring (or shaking the pan frequently), until they just begin to release their fragrance, about 3 to 4 minutes (alternately, preheat oven to 325°F, spread the nuts on an ungreased baking sheet, and bake, stirring often, for 4 to 6 minutes). Remove the nuts from the heat and cool to room temperature. Feel free to improvise on the filling for this cookie.

TO PREPARE COOKIES: In a small bowl, whisk together the flour, baking powder, powdered sugar, salt, cinnamon, and cardamom, and reserve. In the bowl of a food processor fitted with a metal blade, pulse the pecans until the nuts are very finely ground. Whisk the nuts into the flour mixture.

In the bowl of an electric mixer on medium-high speed, beat the butter until creamy, about 1 minute. Add the granulated sugar and beat until light and fluffy, about 2 minutes. Add the egg and vanilla extract and beat until thoroughly combined. Reduce the speed to low, add the flour mixture, and mix just until combined and a dough forms (adding enough milk or water, 1 teaspoon at a time, to make the dough pliable). Form the dough into a disk, wrap in plastic wrap, and refrigerate for at least 2 hours.

When ready to bake, preheat the oven to 375°F and line the baking sheets with parchment paper.

On a lightly floured surface using a lightly floured rolling pin, roll the dough to ⅛-inch thickness. Using a star-shaped cutter (about 3 to 4 inches), cut the dough into stars. Use a smaller star-shaped cutter (about 1 to 2 inches) to cut shapes out of the center of half of the cookies (these will be the top cookies), and place 1 inch apart on the prepared baking sheets. Repeat with the remaining dough, gathering up scraps, re-rolling, and cutting until all the dough is used. Bake until the cookies are just set and beginning to brown, about 8 to 10 minutes. Remove the cookies from the oven and cool for 2 minutes before transferring them to a wire rack to cool completely.

TO PREPARE FILLING: In a saucepan over low heat, combine the apples, cinnamon, nutmeg, cardamom, cloves, brown sugar, and lemon juice, and cook until the apples are soft and can be easily mashed, about 30 to 45 minutes. Pass the mixture through a food mill (or pulse in a food processor fitted with a metal blade) to achieve a smooth consistency. There should be about ½ cup filling.

TO ASSEMBLE COOKIES: Spread 1 teaspoon filling on the flat side of one cookie. Place the flat side of a cutout cookie against the filling, as if making a sandwich. Press gently, just until the filling is at the edge of the cookies. Repeat with the remaining cookies. Dust with powdered sugar (optional).

Cinnamon Cookie-Butter Sandwich Cookies

When Annette Gustafson of Maple Grove first encountered Biscoff Cookie Butter, she became an immediate and enthusiastic fan. "This stuff is so amazing, I've been eating it by the spoonful," she said. "I knew as soon as I had tasted it that I somehow needed to incorporate it into a cookie. I tried incorporating it into the cookie itself, but the flavor didn't come through. That's when I thought, 'What if it was a sandwich cookie, with a Biscoff buttercream filling?'"

MAKES 2 DOZEN COOKIES

FOR CINNAMON SUGAR

1 ¹/₂ teaspoons ground cinnamon

2 tablespoons granulated sugar

FOR COOKIES

2 ¹/₄ cups flour

2 teaspoons ground cinnamon

¹/₄ teaspoon salt

1 cup (2 sticks) unsalted butter, at room temperature

¹/₂ cup packed dark brown sugar

FOR FILLING

6 tablespoons (³/₄ stick) unsalted butter, at room temperature

10 tablespoons (¹/₂ cup plus 2 tablespoons) Biscoff Cookie Butter (see Note)

1 cup powdered sugar

1 to 2 tablespoons heavy cream, at room temperature

NOTE This dough must be prepared in advance. Lotus brand Biscoff Cookie Butter is available in the peanut butter aisle of most supermarkets; Trader Joe's makes a similar product called Trader Joe's Cookie Butter.

TO PREPARE CINNAMON SUGAR: In a small bowl, whisk together cinnamon and granulated sugar, and reserve.

TO PREPARE COOKIES: In a medium bowl, whisk together the flour, 2 teaspoons cinnamon, and salt, and reserve.

In the bowl of an electric mixer on medium-high speed, beat 1 cup butter until creamy, about 1 minute. Add the brown sugar and beat until light and fluffy, about 2 minutes. Reduce the speed to low, add the flour mixture, and mix until just combined and a dough forms (adding enough water, 1 teaspoon at a time, to make the dough pliable). Form the dough into a disk, wrap in plastic wrap, and refrigerate for at least 30 minutes.

When ready to bake, preheat the oven to 300°F and line the baking sheets with parchment paper.

Remove and discard the plastic wrap from the chilled dough. Place the dough between layers of parchment paper. Using a rolling pin, roll the dough to ¹/₄-inch thickness. Using a 2-inch round or fluted cookie cutter, cut the dough into cookies and place 2 inches apart on the prepared baking sheets. Repeat with the remaining dough, gathering up the scraps, re-rolling and cutting until all the dough is used. Sprinkle the cookies with the cinnamon-sugar mixture and bake until the cookies are just lightly golden but not browned around the edges, about 18 to 20 minutes. Remove the cookies from the oven and cool for 2 minutes before transferring them to a wire rack to cool completely.

TO PREPARE FILLING: In the bowl of an electric mixer on medium speed, beat 6 tablespoons butter until creamy and smooth, about 2 minutes. Add the cookie butter and beat until thoroughly combined, about 3 minutes. Reduce the speed to low and gradually add the powdered sugar (the mixture will become somewhat thick). Increase the speed to medium and add 1 tablespoon cream, mixing until a smooth and fluffy consistency is achieved (add more cream, as needed, 1 teaspoon at a time and up to 3 teaspoons).

TO ASSEMBLE COOKIES: Spoon or pipe a dollop of filling into the center of the flat side of one cookie. Place the flat side of a second cookie against the filling, as if making a sandwich. Press gently, just until the filling is at the edge of the cookies. Repeat with the remaining cookies.

Clareos

"I love all kinds of sweets, so I'm always trying new recipes," said Jane Stern of Minneapolis. Her large cookbook collection includes *The Good Cookie* by Tish Boyle, the source of this better-than-Oreos recipe. Jane improved on the original butter-cream filling recipe by replacing Kahlua and vanilla extract with brewed coffee.

MAKES 1 ½ DOZEN COOKIES

FOR COOKIES

1 ¼ cups flour, plus extra for rolling dough

2 teaspoons instant espresso powder

¼ teaspoon salt

¾ cup (1 ½ sticks) unsalted butter, at room temperature

¾ cup granulated sugar

1 egg

1 teaspoon vanilla extract

¾ cup unsweetened Dutch-process cocoa powder

FOR FILLING

3 tablespoons unsalted butter, at room temperature

1 cup plus 2 tablespoons powdered sugar

1 tablespoon strongly brewed coffee, plus extra if filling is too thick

NOTE This dough must be prepared in advance.

TO PREPARE COOKIES: In a medium bowl, whisk together the flour, espresso powder, and salt, and reserve. In the bowl of an electric mixer on medium-high speed, beat the butter until creamy, about 1 minute. Gradually add the granulated sugar and beat until light and fluffy, about 2 minutes. Add the egg and beat until thoroughly combined. Add the vanilla extract and beat until thoroughly combined. Reduce the speed to low and gradually add the cocoa powder, mixing until just combined. Add the flour mixture in three additions, mixing until just combined. Divide the dough into two equal pieces. Form the dough into disks, wrap in plastic wrap, and refrigerate for at least 2 hours or overnight.

When ready to bake, preheat the oven to 325°F and line the baking sheets with parchment paper.

On a lightly floured surface using a lightly floured rolling pin, roll the dough to ¼-inch thickness. Using a 2-inch round or scalloped cookie cutter, cut as many circles as possible and place 1 inch apart on the prepared baking sheets. Repeat with the remaining dough, gathering up the scraps, re-rolling, and cutting until all the dough is used.

Bake the cookies until they no longer look wet and are soft to the touch, 7 to 9 minutes. Remove the cookies from the oven and cool for 2 minutes before transferring them to a wire rack to cool completely.

TO PREPARE FILLING: In the bowl of an electric mixer on medium-high speed, beat the butter until creamy, about 1 minute. Reduce the speed to low and gradually add the powdered sugar. Add the coffee and mix until thoroughly combined (adding more, 1 teaspoon at a time, if necessary to reach the desired consistency). Increase the speed to high and beat until the filling is creamy, about 2 minutes.

TO ASSEMBLE COOKIES: Spoon 1 teaspoon of the filling on the flat side of one cookie. Place the flat side of a second cookie against the filling, as if making a sandwich. Press gently, just until the filling is at the edge of the cookies. Repeat with the remaining cookies.

Peanut Stars

John Halstrom and Trevor Howe of Minneapolis are self-professed peanut lovers. "When I eat peanut butter—which I do, a lot—it reminds me of being a kid," said Halstrom. "My mom always made those Christmas cookies with the Hershey's Kisses." Howe fondly recalls his Massachusetts grandmother's cake-like peanut butter cookies with a peanut–ginger glaze, and Halstrom has great affection for his mother's crisp peanut butter cookies. Borrowing attributes from both, the spouses began experimenting with textures and flavors, scanning websites for guidance, until they hit recipe pay dirt. "I have a ridiculous sweet tooth," said Howe. "What I like about these cookies is that they're not overwhelmingly sweet. Your teeth don't feel like they're rotting out of your head with the first bite."

MAKES 2 DOZEN COOKIES

FOR COOKIES

1 ¼ cups unsalted peanuts, toasted (see Note)

¾ cup flour

1 teaspoon baking soda

½ teaspoon salt

3 tablespoons unsalted butter, melted

½ cup creamy peanut butter (see Note)

½ cup granulated sugar

½ cup packed light brown sugar

3 tablespoons whole milk

1 egg

FOR FILLING

¾ cup creamy peanut butter

3 tablespoons unsalted butter

1 cup powdered sugar

1 teaspoon peeled and freshly grated ginger

NOTE This dough must be prepared in advance. Both raw or roasted peanuts are suitable, and both are better when toasted. To toast, place peanuts in a dry skillet over medium heat, and cook, stirring or shaking the pan frequently, until they just begin to release their fragrance, about 4 to 5 minutes (or preheat the oven to 325°F, spread the nuts on an ungreased baking sheet and bake, stirring often, for 5 to 7 minutes). Remove the nuts from the heat and cool to room temperature. Shelf-stable peanut butter, such as Jif or Skippy, works best, due to its salt and sugar content.

TO PREPARE COOKIES: In a food processor fitted with a metal blade, pulse the peanuts until they are finely chopped and resemble coarse crumbs (alternately, chop peanuts very fine), and reserve. In a medium bowl, whisk together the flour, baking soda, and salt, and reserve.

In the bowl of an electric mixer on medium-high speed, beat the melted butter, peanut butter, granulated sugar, and brown sugar until smooth, about 2 minutes. Add the milk and egg, and beat until thoroughly combined. Reduce the speed to low, add the flour mixture, and mix until just combined. Fold in the peanuts. Cover the bowl with plastic wrap and refrigerate for at least 1 hour.

When ready to bake, preheat the oven to 350°F and line the baking sheets with parchment paper.

Shape the dough into ½-inch balls and place 2 inches apart on the prepared baking sheets. Gently flatten cookies into 1-inch disks. Bake until the edges are slightly browned, 10 to 13 minutes. Remove the

cookies from the oven and cool for 2 minutes before transferring them to a wire rack to cool completely.

TO PREPARE FILLING: Place the peanut butter and butter in a small microwave-safe bowl. Cook until the mixture is easily stirred, about 30 seconds. Add the powdered sugar and ginger, and mix until the filling is smooth.

TO ASSEMBLE COOKIES: Spread 1 teaspoon of the filling on the flat side of one cookie. Place the flat side of a second cookie against the filling, as if making a sandwich. Press gently, just until the filling is at the edge of the cookies. Repeat with the remaining cookies.

Pistachio Orange Cookies

When he's not working, Scott Rohr of St. Paul is baking. "It's sort of a joke with my friends," he said. "I don't remember a time when I haven't baked. I grew up in one of those houses where everything was homemade. Some people come home from work and boil water for dinner. I take out eggs and butter." For his winning recipe, Rohr started with his tattered recipe card for a cream-of-tartar-based sugar cookie, which is a copy of a similarly well-worn card from his grandmother's kitchen. The filling and the pistachios, however, were all his idea. "I just started messing around," he said. "It's really hard for me to follow a recipe. These cookies aren't complicated, and they come together fast. They look like something substantial, but they're not hard to make. If you've ever baked a cookie, then you can bake these, for heaven's sake."

MAKES 3 DOZEN COOKIES

FOR COOKIES

2 cups flour

1 teaspoon salt

2 teaspoons cream of tartar

1 teaspoon baking soda

1 cup (2 sticks) unsalted butter, at room temperature

½ cup granulated sugar, plus extra for rolling dough

½ cup packed light brown sugar

1 egg

1 teaspoon vanilla extract

FOR FILLING

1 cup raw shelled pistachios, divided

½ cup (1 stick) unsalted butter, at room temperature

Freshly grated zest from 1 orange, finely chopped

1 teaspoon orange extract

1 teaspoon vanilla extract

3 cups powdered sugar

2 tablespoons milk (or use 1 tablespoon milk and 1 tablespoon freshly squeezed orange juice)

TO PREPARE COOKIES: Preheat the oven to 350°F and line the baking sheets with parchment paper.

In a medium bowl, whisk together the flour, salt, cream of tartar, and baking soda, and reserve.

In the bowl of an electric mixer on medium-high speed, beat the butter until creamy, about 1 minute. Add the granulated sugar and brown sugar and beat until light and fluffy, about 2 minutes. Add the egg and vanilla extract and beat until thoroughly combined. Reduce the speed to low and add the flour mixture, in three additions, and mix until just combined.

Shape the dough into 1-inch balls. Roll each ball in granulated sugar and place 2 inches apart on the prepared baking sheets. Bake until the cookies are set but not browned, about 11 minutes (the cookies will puff up in the oven, but then flatten). Remove the cookies from the oven and cool for 2 minutes before transferring them to a wire rack to cool completely.

TO PREPARE FILLING: In a food processor fitted with a metal blade, pulse ½ cup pistachios until very fine (the nuts should almost clump together in a paste between your fingers), and reserve.

In the bowl of an electric mixer on medium-high speed, beat the butter with the orange zest until creamy, about 1 minute. Add the orange extract and vanilla extract, and beat until thoroughly combined. Reduce the speed to low. Add the powdered sugar in three additions, alternating with the milk (or milk and orange juice) and beginning and ending with the powdered sugar. Mix until smooth (you may need another tablespoon or so of liquid to reach the desired consistency). Fold in the chopped pistachios and mix until thoroughly combined.

TO ASSEMBLE COOKIES: Finely chop the remaining 1/2 cup pistachios and place in a shallow dish. Spread a generous dollop of the filling on the flat side of one cookie. Place the flat side of a second cookie against the filling, as if making a sandwich. Press gently, just until the filling is at the edge of the cookies. Roll the filled edge in chopped pistachios. Repeat with the remaining cookies.

Red Velvet Whoopie Pies

The father-and-son duo Mike and Nick Burakowski of Golden Valley are serious holiday bakers, turning out twenty varieties of cookies, four cheesecakes, and a parade of Polish and German savory dishes for their annual Christmas party. "We usually spend the week before the party doing a lot of baking," said Mike. "We keep Costco very busy, buying in bulk." They discovered this recipe, an irresistible, bite-sized spin on red velvet cake, in *Southern Living* magazine.

MAKES 2 TO 4 DOZEN COOKIES

FOR COOKIES

2 cups flour

2 tablespoons unsweetened cocoa powder

1/2 teaspoon baking soda

1/4 teaspoon salt

1/2 cup (1 stick) unsalted butter, at room temperature

1 cup packed light brown sugar

1 egg

1 teaspoon vanilla extract

1/2 cup buttermilk

1 (1-ounce) bottle red food coloring

FOR FILLING

4 tablespoons (1/2 stick) unsalted butter, at room temperature

4 ounces cream cheese, at room temperature

1 (7-ounce) jar marshmallow creme

NOTE Yes, the recipe calls for an entire bottle of red food coloring. Be sure to turn off the mixer before adding the food coloring, and mix on low speed.

TO PREPARE COOKIES: Preheat the oven to 375°F and line the baking sheets with parchment paper.

In a medium bowl, whisk together the flour, cocoa powder, baking soda, and salt, and reserve.

In the bowl of an electric mixer on medium-high speed, beat the butter until creamy, about 1 minute. Add the brown sugar and beat until light and fluffy, about 2 minutes.

Add the egg and vanilla extract and beat until thoroughly combined. Reduce the speed to low. Add the flour mixture in three additions, alternating with the buttermilk and beginning and ending with the flour mixture. Mix until just combined. Carefully add the food coloring and mix until thoroughly combined.

Shape the dough into 1-inch balls, and place 2 inches apart on the prepared baking sheets. Bake until the tops are set, about 7 to 9 minutes. Remove the cookies from the oven and cool them completely on the baking sheets.

TO PREPARE FILLING: In the bowl of an electric mixer on medium-high speed, beat the butter and cream cheese until smooth. Add the marshmallow creme and mix until thoroughly combined.

TO ASSEMBLE COOKIES: Spread a generous dollop of the filling on the flat side of one cookie. Place the flat side of a second cookie against the filling, as if making a sandwich. Press gently, just until the filling is at the edge of the cookies. Repeat with the remaining cookies. Cover and refrigerate.

Rosemary Lemon Creams

For Cynthia Baxter of Minneapolis, buttery shortbreads are her cookie of choice, especially when they're formed into sandwiches filled with an uncomplicated butter-cream icing. "I've made them a million times," she said. A friend's rosemary-scented shortbread inspired Baxter to explore the savory side of her favorite cookie, which she embellished with brown sugar and lemon flourishes. This elegant recipe was Baxter's second appearance in the contest; previously, she had been a finalist with her Marzipan Almond Shortbread. "And every year after that, I probably receive at least ten emails from friends asking, 'What are you going to enter this year?'" she said. "It's the cutest thing."

MAKES 2 DOZEN COOKIES

FOR ROSEMARY BROWN SUGAR

1 large fresh rosemary sprig
3/4 cup packed light brown sugar

FOR COOKIES

2 cups flour, plus more for rolling dough
1/4 teaspoon salt
1/4 teaspoon baking powder
1 cup (2 sticks) unsalted butter, at room
    temperature
1 teaspoon freshly grated lemon zest
1 teaspoon finely chopped fresh rosemary
Fresh small rosemary leaves, for garnish

FOR LEMON CREAM

2 cups sifted powdered sugar, plus more as
    needed
1/4 teaspoon salt
2 tablespoons unsalted butter, at room
    temperature
1/3 cup mascarpone cheese
2 tablespoons freshly squeezed lemon juice,
    plus more as needed

NOTE This dough must be prepared in advance.

TO PREPARE ROSEMARY BROWN SUGAR: Gently roll the rosemary sprig between your hands or under a rolling pin to release its fragrance. In a small bowl or jar, bury the rosemary in the brown sugar, cover tightly and let sit at room temperature for 24 to 72 hours; the longer it sits, the deeper the flavor. When ready to bake, discard the rosemary sprig from the brown sugar and reserve the brown sugar.

TO PREPARE COOKIES: In a medium bowl, whisk together the flour, salt, and baking powder, and reserve.

In the bowl of an electric mixer on medium-high speed, beat the butter and 1/2 cup packed rosemary brown sugar (reserving remaining 1/4 cup rosemary brown sugar) until light and fluffy, about 2 minutes.

Reduce the speed to low, add the flour mixture, and mix until just combined. Add the lemon zest and 1 teaspoon finely chopped rosemary, and mix until just combined. Form the dough into a disk, wrap in plastic wrap, and refrigerate for 1 hour.

When ready to bake, preheat the oven to 350°F and line the baking sheets with parchment paper.

On a lightly floured surface using a lightly floured rolling pin, roll the dough to 1/4-inch thickness. Using a small cookie cutter, cut the dough into cookie shapes and place 2 inches apart on the prepared baking sheets. Repeat with the remaining dough, gathering up the scraps, re-rolling and cutting until all the dough is used.

For half of the cookies, lightly brush the tops with water (leaving the other half of the cookies plain). Sprinkle the remaining ¼ cup rosemary brown sugar on the water-brushed cookies and then garnish with small rosemary leaves. Bake until the cookies are lightly browned on the bottom, about 12 to 14 minutes. Remove the cookies from the oven and cool for 2 minutes before transferring them to a wire rack to cool completely.

TO PREPARE LEMON CREAM: In the bowl of an electric mixer on low speed, combine the powdered sugar, salt, butter, mascarpone, and lemon juice, and mix until combined. Increase the speed to medium and mix until the cream is smooth and creamy, adjusting with powdered sugar or lemon juice to achieve desired consistency.

TO ASSEMBLE COOKIES: Spoon or pipe a dollop of the lemon cream into the center of the flat side of a plain cookie. Place the flat side of a rosemary-topped cookie against the first cookie, as if making a sandwich. Press gently, just until the lemon cream is at the edge of the cookie. Repeat with the remaining cookies.

CONTENTS

CHAPTER TWO

Drop Cookies

Acorn Cookies

When Barbara Melom of Minneapolis moved to Minnesota from Pennsylvania in the late 1960s, she was taken with the cookie traditions she found in her new home state: krumkake, sandbakkels, and other delicate delicacies. "In Pennsylvania we baked sturdy cookies," she said. "Lots of raisins and nuts, really dense and heavy." When the calendar rolls around to Christmas baking, Melom adheres to one rule: no rolling pins. This is one reason why the retired speech therapist has been making Acorn Cookies for decades: they look complicated, but they're just two easy steps beyond a simple drop cookie. They're one of eight to ten varieties that Melom bakes each December, when she showers her friends and acquaintances with cookies. "If you ask me, a cup of coffee and a good cookie is one of life's simple pleasures," she said.

MAKES 3 DOZEN COOKIES

FOR COOKIES

1 cup (2 sticks) unsalted butter
3/4 cup packed dark brown sugar
1 teaspoon vanilla extract
1/3 cup finely chopped pecans
2 1/2 cups flour
1/2 teaspoon baking powder

FOR CARAMEL COATING

1 (11-ounce) package caramels (such as
   the Kraft brand), unwrapped
3/4 cup chopped pecans

TO PREPARE COOKIES: Preheat the oven to 350°F and line the baking sheets with parchment paper.

In a medium saucepan over low heat, melt the butter. Remove the pan from the heat, transfer the butter to a large bowl, and stir in the brown sugar, vanilla extract, and pecans.

In a medium bowl, whisk together the flour and baking powder. Add the flour mixture to the butter mixture and mix until thoroughly combined.

Shape the dough into 1-inch balls, and place 2 inches apart on the prepared baking sheets. Flatten the balls on the bottoms and pinch the tops to form a point so the dough resembles an acorn. Bake until golden brown, 15 to 18 minutes. Remove the cookies from the oven and cool for 2 minutes before transferring them to a wire rack to cool completely.

TO PREPARE CARAMEL COATING: In a double boiler over gently simmering water (or in a bowl in a microwave oven), combine the caramels and 2 tablespoons water. Heat until the caramels melt, stirring occasionally; if too thick, thin the mixture with water, 1 teaspoon at a time, until the caramel coating reaches spreading consistency. Remove from the heat but keep the caramel coating warm over hot water.

Dip the flat side of each cookie into the caramel coating, allowing the excess to drop off, and then into the chopped pecans. Place the cookies on wax paper or parchment paper and allow the caramel coating to set before serving.

Bacon Cornmeal Venetos

High school friends Julie Bollmann of Chanhassen, Wendy Kleiser of Minneapolis, Joan Koller of Jordan, Geri Olson of Shoreview, and Mary Urbas of Woodbury gather for an annual cookie bake and exchange. "We call ourselves the Cookie Chicks," said Bollmann, noting that the club also includes matching aprons and recipe scrapbooks. "Now a couple of daughters are participating—we call them the Chicklets." Bollmann always test-drives a few recipes from the *Star Tribune* Holiday Cookie Contest, and she proposed that they submit a recipe. She assures first-timers that this drop cookie is easy. "If I can make it, anyone can," she said with a laugh. "Besides, bacon in a cookie is a good excuse to have cookies for breakfast."

MAKES 3 TO 4 DOZEN COOKIES

FOR COOKIES

¾ cup golden raisins

1 cup finely ground yellow cornmeal

1 ½ cups flour

1 ½ teaspoons baking powder

Pinch of salt

1 cup (2 sticks) unsalted butter, at room temperature

6 tablespoons maple syrup

2 eggs

1 teaspoon vanilla extract

4 bacon strips, cooked and chopped into small pieces, about ½ cup

FOR BROWN BUTTER

1 tablespoon unsalted butter

FOR GLAZE

1 cup powdered sugar

¼ teaspoon maple extract

2 tablespoons milk

NOTE Maple extract is used in the glaze to bump up its flavor. For the cookie dough, use real maple syrup.

TO PREPARE COOKIES: Preheat the oven to 350°F and line the baking sheets with parchment paper. Place a wire rack over wax paper or parchment paper.

In a small bowl, cover the raisins with warm water and soak for 15 minutes. Strain, reserving the raisins. In a medium bowl, whisk together the cornmeal, flour, baking powder, and salt, and reserve.

In the bowl of an electric mixer on medium-high speed, cream the butter and maple syrup until light and fluffy, about 2 minutes. Add the eggs, one at a time, beating well after each addition. Add the vanilla extract and beat until thoroughly combined. Reduce the speed to low, add the flour mixture, and mix until just combined. Stir in the raisins and bacon.

Shape the dough into 1-inch balls, and place 2 inches apart on the prepared baking sheets. Bake until golden brown on the edges, about 10 minutes. Remove the cookies from the oven and cool for 2 minutes before transferring them to a wire rack to cool completely.

TO PREPARE BROWN BUTTER: In a medium saucepan over medium heat, melt the butter, stirring constantly, until the butter smells nutty and browned bits begin to form at the bottom of the pan, about 5 minutes. Remove from the heat.

TO PREPARE GLAZE: Add the powdered sugar, maple extract, and milk to the brown butter, and whisk until the glaze is smooth and a single consistent color. Drizzle the glaze over the cookies. Allow the glaze to set before serving.

Brandy Cherry Cookies

Kathleen Sonsteng of Laporte found this recipe in *Country Home* magazine, and she reserves it for December. "A few years ago, I gave the recipe to a friend, who now makes them year-round," she said. "But I keep it special and only make them on the holidays. As soon as I made this recipe for the first time, in 2008, it became a Christmas standard. It has become a tradition in our house, and I give it to others, because everyone loves it."

MAKES 3 DOZEN COOKIES

1 cup dried cherries
½ cup brandy
2 ½ cups flour, plus extra if needed
¼ teaspoon salt
½ teaspoon five-spice powder (see Note)
1 cup (2 sticks) unsalted butter, at room temperature
1 cup granulated sugar, divided
1 egg
1 egg yolk

NOTE This dough must be prepared in advance. Five-spice powder is a blend of equal parts cinnamon, cloves, fennel seed, star anise, and Szechuan peppercorns. You can find it in the spice aisle of most supermarkets. If the cherries are large, chop them. Don't overwork this dough, or you may end up with flattened cookies.

In a small saucepan over medium heat, combine the dried cherries and brandy. When the brandy starts to simmer, remove the pan from the heat and let stand for 30 minutes. Drain, reserving both the cherries and the liquid.

In a medium bowl, whisk together the flour, salt, and five-spice powder, and reserve. In the bowl of an electric mixer on medium-high speed, beat the butter until light and fluffy, about 1 minute. Add ¾ cup granulated sugar and beat until thoroughly combined, about 2 minutes. Add the egg, egg yolk, and 2 teaspoons of the reserved brandy liquid

(discard the remaining liquid), and beat until thoroughly combined. Reduce the speed to low, add the flour mixture, and mix until just combined (if the dough is sticky, add more flour, 1 tablespoon at a time; you need to be able to roll the dough into balls in your hands). Stir in the drained cherries. Shape the dough into 1-inch balls, and refrigerate for at least 2 hours, or overnight.

When ready to bake, preheat the oven to 350°F and line the baking sheets with parchment paper.

Place the remaining ¼ cup granulated sugar in a shallow bowl. Roll the cookies in the granulated sugar to coat and place 1 inch apart on the prepared baking sheets. Bake until lightly browned and set on the edges, about 10 to 12 minutes. Remove the cookies from the oven and cool for 2 minutes before transferring them to a wire rack to cool completely.

Buttery Blueberry Buttons

Carla McClellan of Minneapolis pulls her fair share of kitchen duty with her fellow firefighters, but she didn't seek any feedback from her colleagues for this delicate cookie. "I don't know that fruit is a favorite part of any meal for them," she said with a laugh. Dried cherries, apricots, or other fruits also work very well in this easy-to-prepare recipe, which grew out of a formula that McClellan encountered at a baking-centric website and tweaked. "Having fun and experimenting is the best part of baking," she said. "I always have music playing on my phone when I'm in the kitchen. Doesn't everyone have a soundtrack when they're baking?"

MAKES 2 DOZEN COOKIES

1/2 cup salted butter (1 stick), at room
     temperature
1/3 cup granulated sugar
1/4 teaspoon baking soda
1 tablespoon vanilla extract
1 egg yolk
1 cup flour
1/2 cup dried blueberries (see Note)
Powdered sugar, for garnish

NOTE   Find dried blueberries in the dried fruits section at many supermarkets and the bulk foods sections of many natural foods co-ops. Consider adding 1/2 teaspoon freshly grated lemon zest when adding the dried blueberries to the dough.

Preheat the oven to 350°F and line the baking sheets with parchment paper.

In the bowl of an electric mixer on medium speed, beat the butter until creamy, about 1 minute. Add the granulated sugar and beat until light and fluffy, about 2 minutes. Sprinkle the baking soda over the mixture and beat until thoroughly combined. Then add the vanilla extract and egg yolk, and beat until thoroughly combined. Reduce the speed to low and add the flour, a few tablespoons at a time, mixing until just combined. Stir in the dried blueberries.

Shape the dough into 1-inch balls, and place 2 inches apart on the prepared baking sheets. Bake until the cookies are lightly browned on the bottom, about 8 minutes. Place a wire rack over wax paper or parchment paper. Remove the cookies from the oven and cool for 2 minutes before transferring them to the prepared wire rack to cool completely. Dust with powdered sugar.

Candy Cane Sugar Cookies

When Michelle Mazzara of Eagan was creating this recipe, she kept returning to her Italian grandmother for inspiration. "She was happiest when she was cooking," said Mazzara. "She would bake for two or three months before Christmas, and she would give boxes and boxes of cookies to everyone she knew." Which explains why Mazzara started with Grandma Rose's sugar cookie recipe. "They just sort of melted in your mouth," she said. As for the minty fresh flourish: "The scent of peppermint is very vivid in my mind when I think about Christmas."

MAKES 4 DOZEN COOKIES

FOR COOKIES

2 ½ cups flour
1 teaspoon baking soda
½ teaspoon cream of tartar
¼ teaspoon salt
1 cup (2 sticks) unsalted butter, at room
    temperature
1 ¼ cups granulated sugar
3 egg yolks
1 teaspoon vanilla extract
1 teaspoon peppermint extract
1 cup (about 6 ounces) crushed candy canes
    or peppermint hard candies (see Note)

FOR ICING

½ cup (1 stick) unsalted butter, at room
    temperature
4 ounces cream cheese, at room temperature
1 teaspoon peppermint extract
2 cups powdered sugar
⅛ teaspoon salt
2 drops red food coloring

NOTE For easier cleanup after crushing the peppermint candy, consider using a paper or plastic bag, or lining the top of a cutting board with parchment paper or wax paper, and covering the candy with the same.

TO PREPARE COOKIES: Preheat the oven to 350°F and line the baking sheets with parchment paper.

In a medium bowl, whisk together the flour, baking soda, cream of tartar, and salt, and reserve.

In the bowl of an electric mixer on medium-high speed, beat the butter until creamy, about 1 minute. Add the granulated sugar, and beat until light and fluffy, about 2 minutes. Add the egg yolks, one at a time, beating well after each addition. Add the vanilla extract and peppermint extract, and beat until well combined. Reduce the speed to low, add the flour mixture, and mix until just combined. Stir in the candy pieces.

Shape the dough into 1-inch balls, and place 2 inches apart on the prepared baking sheets. Bake until tops are cracked and lightly browned, about 11 to 13 minutes. Remove the cookies from the oven and cool for 2 minutes before transferring them to a wire rack to cool completely.

TO PREPARE ICING: In the bowl of an electric mixer on medium speed, combine the butter, cream cheese, and peppermint extract, and beat until creamy. Reduce the speed to low, add the powdered sugar and salt, and mix until creamy. Add the food coloring, 1 drop at a time, to reach desired color. Spread the icing on the cookies. Allow the icing to set before serving.

Cardamom Cherry Buttons

The key ingredient to this brown butter-enriched cookie is Luxardo brand maraschino cherries. They're an Italian import, and they improve everything they touch, especially cocktails. And now, cookies. "I was introduced to them a few years ago by a friend who was making Old Fashioneds with them," said Tammy Meyerhofer of Sartell. "They were so good, so intensely flavorful, and such a treat when you got to the bottom of the glass. I don't know where I got the idea to bring them out from behind the bar and into the kitchen, but it works."

MAKES 4 ½ DOZEN COOKIES

FOR BROWN BUTTER

1 cup (2 sticks) unsalted butter

FOR COOKIES

3 ¼ cups flour

¾ teaspoon baking powder

½ teaspoon baking soda

¼ teaspoon salt

1 teaspoon ground cardamom

1 ¼ cups granulated sugar

2 eggs

¼ cup light corn syrup

Sparkling sugar or other decorative sugars

1 (14.1 ounce) jar Luxardo brand maraschino cherries, drained (see Note)

NOTE This dough must be prepared in advance. Luxardo brand maraschino cherries, imported from Italy, are available at most liquor stores and some specialty foods stores. For a less-expensive option, substitute any premium cocktail cherry, or use standard maraschino cherries or even tart cherries, soaking them overnight in a flavorful liqueur.

TO PREPARE BROWN BUTTER: In a medium saucepan over medium heat, melt the butter and cook, stirring constantly, until the butter smells nutty and becomes a deep golden color, and browned bits begin to form at the bottom of the pan, about 5 minutes. Remove from the heat, transfer the brown butter to a small bowl and cool to room temperature.

TO PREPARE COOKIES: In a medium bowl, whisk together the flour, baking powder, baking soda, salt, and cardamom, and reserve.

In the bowl of an electric mixer on medium speed, beat the brown butter and granulated sugar until light and fluffy, about 2 to 3 minutes. Add the eggs, one at a time, beating until thoroughly combined. Add the corn syrup, and beat until light and fluffy. Reduce the speed to low, add the flour mixture, and mix until just combined. Cover with plastic wrap and refrigerate the dough for at least 1 hour, or overnight.

When ready to bake, preheat the oven to 375°F and line the baking sheets with parchment paper.

Place the sparkling sugar in a shallow bowl. Shape the dough into 1-inch balls. Roll the cookies in the sparkling sugar to coat and place 2 inches apart on the prepared baking sheets. Bake until the tops of the cookies are puffed and edges are set, about 6 to 8 minutes. Remove the cookies from the oven and immediately top with a maraschino cherry. Cool the cookies for 2 minutes before transferring them to a wire rack to cool completely.

Cardamom Cookies

Matt Boisen of Owatonna found inspiration for these chewy, brightly flavored cookies after a trip to Denmark during the holidays. "Cardamom and marzipan were two things you smelled everywhere," he said. Later he saw a recipe in a Danish cookbook that reminded him of his aunt Beverly's frosted spice holiday cookies, but with the addition of cardamom. "I know a lot of people run away from cardamom," said Boisen with a laugh. "But to me, it's intoxicating. I like to try something different. They're not like chocolate chip cookies. That's all my mom ever made, and I got burned out on them. No one can convince me to ever have another one of those."

MAKES 4 DOZEN COOKIES

FOR COOKIES

1/2 teaspoon baking soda

1 teaspoon ground cardamom

1 teaspoon ground cinnamon

1 1/2 cups flour

1/2 cup (1 stick) unsalted butter, at room temperature

1 cup granulated sugar

1 egg

FOR ICING

4 tablespoons (1/2 stick) unsalted butter, at room temperature

1 teaspoon vanilla extract

1/2 cup milk

1/2 teaspoon ground cardamom

1/2 teaspoon ground cinnamon

4 cups powdered sugar

TO PREPARE COOKIES: Preheat the oven to 350°F and line the baking sheets with parchment paper. In a small bowl, whisk together the baking soda, cardamom, cinnamon, and flour, and reserve.

In the bowl of an electric mixer on medium-high speed, beat the butter until creamy, about 1 minute. Add the granulated sugar and beat until light and fluffy, about 2 minutes. Add the egg and beat until thoroughly combined. Reduce the speed to low, add the flour mixture, and mix until just combined.

Shape the dough into 1-inch balls, and place 2 inches apart on the prepared baking sheets. Carefully press the dough with the flat bottom of a glass and bake until lightly browned, 14 to 16 minutes. Remove the cookies from the oven and cool for 2 minutes before transferring them to a wire rack to cool completely.

TO PREPARE ICING: In the bowl of an electric mixer on medium-high speed, beat the butter and vanilla extract until light and fluffy, about 1 minute. Add the milk, cardamom, and cinnamon, and beat well. Reduce the speed to low and add the powdered sugar to reach desired consistency. Spread the icing on the cookies. Allow the icing to set before serving.

Cardamom Crescents

Jingle bell season or not, there is always something delicious filling the cookie jar in Leslie Smith's kitchen in Minneapolis. "Cookies are my weakness," she said. In December, that means Cardamom Crescents. Smith ran across the recipe in a magazine and modified it to suit her family's tastes, jokingly labeling the not-so-sweet biscotti-like treat a "fusion" cookie. The cardamom recalls her and her husband's Scandinavian background and also reflects the Indian heritage of their three adopted children, who love to pitch in when she's baking. "They fight over who gets to help," she said. "They know that they get to sample."

MAKE 5 DOZEN COOKIES

1 teaspoon instant espresso powder

1 teaspoon ground cardamom

1/2 teaspoon baking powder

1 3/4 cups flour

1/2 cup (1 stick) unsalted butter, at room temperature

1 cup granulated sugar

2 cups finely ground hazelnuts or blanched almonds, divided

2 eggs

1 cup semisweet chocolate chips

NOTE This dough must be prepared in advance.

In a medium bowl, whisk together the instant espresso powder, cardamom, baking powder, and flour, and reserve. In the bowl of an electric mixer on medium-high speed, beat the butter until creamy, about 1 minute. Add the granulated sugar and beat until light and fluffy, about 2 minutes. Add 1 cup of the ground hazelnuts or almonds and beat until thoroughly combined. Add the eggs, one at a time, beating well after each addition. Reduce the speed to low, add the flour mixture, and mix until just combined. Cover the bowl with plastic wrap and refrigerate for at least 1 hour.

When ready to bake, preheat the oven to 350°F and line the baking sheets with parchment paper. Place a wire rack over wax paper or parchment paper.

Form the dough into 1-inch balls, shape the dough balls into crescents, and place 1 inch apart on the prepared baking sheets. Bake until the edges are golden brown, 12 to 15 minutes. Remove the cookies from the oven and cool for 2 minutes before transferring them to a wire rack to cool completely.

In a double boiler over gently simmering water (or in a bowl in a microwave oven), melt the chocolate, whisking occasionally until smooth. Quickly dip one end of each crescent into chocolate and then into the remaining 1 cup of chopped nuts. Transfer the cookies to the prepared wire rack and cool until the chocolate sets.

Cardamom Orange Sugar Cookies

The roots for this easy-to-prepare recipe reach back to Jeanne Nordstrom's childhood in Wadena. "People traded recipes, and a neighbor gave this one to Mom," said Nordstrom, who now lives in St. Paul. "Mom made rolled-out sugar cookies, but these were much easier." The idea of infusing this beloved sugar cookie with cardamom and orange accents occurred to Nordstrom, and a taste test at a get-together of high school friends confirmed her suspicions. "I always bring cookies," she said. "They loved this updated version." Contest judges concurred. "It's a Christmas cookie that everyone will want to bake," said one. "It tastes like the holidays," added another. "It looks like a snickerdoodle, but then it has that surprise orange–cardamom flavor," observed a third.

MAKES 3 DOZEN COOKIES

FOR COOKIES

2 cups plus 2 tablespoons flour

½ teaspoon salt

½ teaspoon baking soda

½ cup (1 stick) unsalted butter, at room temperature

½ cup granulated sugar

½ cup powdered sugar

½ cup canola oil

1 egg

½ teaspoon vanilla extract

Freshly grated zest from 2 oranges

1 teaspoon ground cardamom

FOR DECORATION

1 ½ tablespoons granulated sugar

½ teaspoon ground cardamom

Unsalted butter, at room temperature

Freshly grated zest from 1 orange, optional

NOTE This dough must be prepared in advance. As the cookies cooled, we decorated them with freshly grated orange zest for additional flavor and color.

TO PREPARE COOKIES: In a medium bowl, whisk together the flour, salt, and baking soda, and reserve. In the bowl of an electric mixer on medium-high speed, beat the butter, granulated sugar, and powdered sugar until light and fluffy, about 2 minutes. Add the canola oil, egg, vanilla extract, orange zest, and cardamom, and beat until thoroughly combined. Reduce the speed to low, add the flour mixture, and mix until just combined. Cover the bowl with plastic wrap and refrigerate for at least 1 hour.

When ready to bake, preheat the oven to 350°F and line the baking sheets with parchment paper.

TO DECORATE COOKIES: In a small bowl, stir together the granulated sugar and cardamom. Shape the dough into 1-inch balls, and place 2 inches apart on the prepared baking sheets. Spread a light coating of butter on the flat bottom of a glass, dip it into the sugar–cardamom mixture, and carefully press the prepared glass bottom into a cookie, flattening it; repeat with the remaining cookies. Bake until the bottom of the cookies are golden brown, about 10 to 12 minutes. Remove the cookies from the oven and cool for 2 minutes before transferring them to a wire rack to cool completely. Sprinkle with the orange zest (optional).

Cashew Lemon Shortbread Cookies

Although Jean Livingood of Detroit Lakes has been making Cashew Lemon Short-bread Cookies for a short time, they've hit number one on her family's cookie roster of greatest hits. Not just at Christmas, either. Her oldest daughter unearthed the recipe in an old cookbook, and everywhere she took them the reaction was the same: wow! At a recent birthday party, the shortbread was quickly reduced to a few crumbs, the only food item completely gone by the end of the event. "That happens everywhere we take them," Livingood said. Besides their simple goodness and easy-to-follow instructions, there's another reason why Livingood has added these newcomers to her baking mix. "I'm a chocolate freak," she said. "And my daughters say, 'Mom, we can't make everything chocolate.'"

MAKES 3 DOZEN COOKIES

1 cup (2 sticks) unsalted butter, at room temperature, plus extra for pressing dough

¾ cup granulated sugar, divided

1 teaspoon lemon extract (or 1 teaspoon freshly squeezed lemon juice and freshly grated lemon zest)

1 teaspoon vanilla extract

2 cups flour

½ cup roasted cashews, chopped

Freshly grated lemon zest, optional

Preheat the oven to 325°F and line the baking sheets with parchment paper.

In the bowl of an electric mixer on medium-high speed, beat the butter until creamy, about 1 minute. Gradually add ½ cup granulated sugar and beat until light and fluffy, about 2 minutes. Add the lemon extract (or lemon juice and lemon zest) and vanilla extract, and beat until thoroughly combined. Reduce the speed to low, add the flour, and mix just until the dough begins to form a ball. Stir in the cashews.

Place the remaining ¼ cup granulated sugar in a shallow bowl. Shape the dough into 1-inch balls. Roll the cookies in the granulated sugar to coat and place 2 inches apart on the prepared baking sheets. Spread a light coating of butter on the flat bottom of a glass, dip it into the granulated sugar, and carefully press the prepared glass bottom into a cookie, flattening it, and sprinkle with a bit of the freshly grated lemon zest (optional); repeat with remaining cookies. Bake just until cookies are set and edges are lightly browned, 17 to 19 minutes. Remove the cookies from the oven and cool for 2 minutes before transferring them to a wire rack to cool completely.

Chocolate Decadence Cookies

"This is the first contest I've ever entered," said Elaine Prebonich of New Brighton. "I love to bake. I'm retired. I have the time." She found the recipe in the newspaper years ago, "and then I've been tweaking it along the way," she said. "It's an absolute favorite, every time I make it." Judges agreed. "'Decadence' is right," was one comment. "Every cookie platter needs chocolate, and these sure pack a chocolate wallop," was another.

MAKES 2 DOZEN COOKIES

2 eggs

½ cup granulated sugar

1 teaspoon vanilla extract

¼ cup flour

¼ teaspoon baking powder

⅛ teaspoon salt

8 ounces bittersweet chocolate, coarsely chopped

2 tablespoons unsalted butter

1 ½ cups coarsely chopped walnuts or other nuts, toasted, if desired (see Note)

6 ounces semisweet chocolate chips

NOTE The amounts of flour and bittersweet chocolate are correctly indicated here. For added flavor, we toasted the walnuts. To toast walnuts, place the nuts in a dry skillet over medium heat and cook, stirring (or shaking the pan frequently), until they just begin to release their fragrance, about 3 to 4 minutes (alternately, preheat oven to 325°F, spread the nuts on an ungreased baking sheet, and bake, stirring often, for 4 to 6 minutes). Remove the nuts from the heat and cool to room temperature. This recipe works well when substituting gluten-free flour for all-purpose flour.

Preheat the oven to 350°F and line the baking sheets with parchment paper.

In a small bowl, whisk together the eggs, granulated sugar, and vanilla extract. Set the bowl in a larger bowl of hot tap water.

In a small bowl, whisk together the flour, baking powder, and salt, and reserve.

In a double boiler over gently simmering water (or in a bowl in a microwave oven), combine the bittersweet chocolate and butter, whisking occasionally until smooth. Remove from the heat and stir in the egg mixture until thoroughly combined. Stir in the flour mixture. Stir in the walnuts and chocolate chips.

Shape the dough into 1-inch balls, and place 2 inches apart on the prepared baking sheets. Bake until the surface looks dry and the centers are still gooey, about 10 minutes. Remove the cookies from the oven and cool for 2 minutes before transferring them to a wire rack to cool completely.

Chocolate-Dipped Triple Coconut Haystacks

Ron Traxinger of St. Louis Park doesn't like to follow recipes. "I'll try it once, and then I'll change it," he said. He ran across a recipe for coconut haystacks in a magazine and, true to form, immediately began to tinker with it. The result? An attention-grabber. "When you put them on a platter with other cookies, they're the first ones to go," he said. "They're elegant and sexy. People want to touch them. They're a better version of any macaroon you've tasted in the past." Most of the batches of haystacks that Traxinger prepares will end up as gifts. "But not for the office," he said with a laugh. "They're too good for the office."

MAKES 2 DOZEN COOKIES

1 cup coconut milk (not cream of coconut)

1/4 cup granulated sugar

2 tablespoons light corn syrup

4 egg whites

2 teaspoons vanilla extract

1/2 teaspoon salt

3 cups shredded coconut, desiccated (dried) and unsweetened

3 cups sweetened shredded coconut

14 ounces semisweet chocolate

NOTE For extra flavor to these gluten-free cookies, add lightly roasted, roughly chopped macadamia nuts (about 3/4 cup) into the final coconut mixture, dropping the cookies into mounds rather than forming haystacks.

Preheat the oven to 375°F and line the baking sheets with parchment paper.

In a medium bowl, whisk together the coconut milk, granulated sugar, corn syrup, egg whites, vanilla extract, and salt. In a large bowl, combine the unsweetened coconut and sweetened coconut, breaking apart any lumps. Pour the coconut milk mixture into the coconut mixture, and stir until the dough is evenly moistened. Cover the bowl in plastic wrap and refrigerate for 15 minutes.

Shape the dough into 1-inch balls, and place on the prepared baking sheets. Form the cookies into haystacks, moistening your fingers with water if necessary. Bake until light-golden brown, about 15 minutes. Remove the cookies from the oven and cool for 2 minutes before transferring them to a wire rack to cool completely.

In a double boiler over gently simmering water (or in a bowl in a microwave oven), melt the chocolate, whisking occasionally until smooth. Place the wire racks over wax paper.

Holding a cooled cookie by its pointed top, carefully dip the bottom of the haystack into melted chocolate, covering up to one-third of the sides of the cookie. Use chopsticks or a fork to remove the cookie, draining off excess chocolate. Place the cookies, chocolate-side down, on the prepared wire racks. Refrigerate until the chocolate sets, about 30 minutes.

Chocolate Peppermint Cookies

For years, Karen Evans of Minneapolis has been baking gigantic amounts of holiday cookies as a gift-giving gesture for her husband's coworkers. "Who doesn't like home-made cookies?" she said. "Every year I try to bake a couple of new kinds, to add to the old favorites." Evans began making this festive cookie—a variation on a recipe she encountered in the pages of the *Cincinnati Enquirer*—decades ago. It quickly became her family's all-time favorite. Our judges agreed. "Kids are going to love this," was the near-unanimous chorus of praise. Evans values finicky-free recipes. "These cookies look sophisticated, but they're actually really easy to make," she said. "And if there are any flaws, you're going to cover them in icing and roll them in crushed candy canes."

MAKES 2 DOZEN COOKIES

FOR COOKIES

1 1/2 cups flour

1/2 cup unsweetened cocoa powder

1/4 teaspoon salt

1/4 teaspoon baking powder

1/4 teaspoon baking soda

1/2 cup (1 stick) unsalted butter, at room temperature

1 cup granulated sugar

1 egg

1 1/2 teaspoons vanilla extract

FOR TOPPING

3 tablespoons unsalted butter, at room temperature

2 cups powdered sugar

1 teaspoon peppermint extract

1 to 3 tablespoons milk (or heavy cream)

1/3 cup crushed hard peppermint candies, such as candy canes (see Note)

NOTE For easier cleanup after crushing the peppermint candy, consider using a paper or plastic bag, or lining the top of a cutting board with parchment paper or wax paper, and covering the candy with the same.

TO PREPARE COOKIES: Preheat the oven to 350°F and line the baking sheets with parchment paper.

In a medium bowl, whisk together the flour, cocoa powder, salt, baking powder, and baking soda, and reserve.

In the bowl of an electric mixer on medium-high speed, beat the butter until creamy, about 1 minute. Add the granulated sugar and beat until light and fluffy, about 2 minutes. Add the egg and vanilla extract, and beat until thoroughly combined. Reduce the speed to low, add the flour mixture, and mix until just combined.

Shape the dough into 1-inch balls, and place 2 inches apart on the prepared baking sheets, flattening the dough slightly. Bake until the cookies are set and look dry, about 10 minutes. Remove the cookies from the oven and cool for 2 minutes before transferring them to a wire rack to cool completely.

TO PREPARE TOPPING: In the bowl of an electric mixer on medium speed, combine the butter and powdered sugar, and beat until creamy. Add the peppermint extract and enough milk (or cream), 1 tablespoon at a time, to achieve a smooth mixture. Spread the icing on the cookies; then press the cookie top into the crushed candy. Allow the icing to set before serving.

Chocolate Toffee Cookies

"I loved Heath bars when I was growing up," said Bonnie Coffey of Pequot Lakes. "Normally, when I look at a cookie recipe, I look at the ratios of fat, flour, and eggs. But this one? It was the toffee component and all of that bittersweet chocolate." She's also a fan of Deb Perelman's Smitten Kitchen blog (smittenkitchen.com), and that's where she first encountered this *Bon Appétit* magazine recipe. "People like chocolate," she said. "It's always going to be a home run."

MAKES 4 DOZEN COOKIES

½ cup flour
1 teaspoon baking powder
½ teaspoon salt
1 pound bittersweet or semisweet chocolate, chopped
4 tablespoons (½ stick) unsalted butter
1 ¾ cup packed light brown sugar
4 eggs
1 tablespoon vanilla extract
5 (1.4 ounce) chocolate-covered English toffee bars (such as Heath), coarsely chopped, or 7 ounces Heath bits
1 cup chopped walnuts, toasted (see Note)
Flaky sea salt for garnish, optional

NOTE This dough must be prepared in advance. To toast walnuts, place the nuts in a dry skillet over medium heat and cook, stirring (or shaking the pan frequently), until they just begin to release their fragrance, about 3 to 4 minutes (alternately, preheat oven to 325°F, spread the nuts on an ungreased baking sheet, and bake, stirring often, for 4 to 6 minutes). The amount of flour is correctly indicated here. And, although the salt is optional, it does create a salty-and-sweet taste that is just a bit different on your cookie plate. This recipe works well when substituting gluten-free flour for all-purpose flour.

In a medium bowl, whisk together the flour, baking powder, and salt, and reserve. In a double boiler over gently simmering water (or in a bowl in a microwave oven), combine the bittersweet (or semisweet) chocolate and butter, whisking occasionally until smooth. Remove from the heat and cool until the mixture is lukewarm.

In the bowl of an electric mixer on medium speed, beat the brown sugar and eggs until thick, about 5 minutes. Reduce the speed to low, add the chocolate mixture and vanilla extract, and mix until well combined. Add the flour mixture until just combined. Stir in the toffee and walnuts. Cover the bowl with plastic wrap and refrigerate for 30 minutes.

When ready to bake, preheat the oven to 350°F and line the baking sheets with parchment paper.

Shape the dough into 1-inch balls, and place 2 inches apart on the prepared baking sheets. Garnish each cookie with a pinch of sea salt (optional). Bake until the tops of the cookies are dry and cracked but are still soft to the touch, about 12 to 14 minutes. Remove the cookies from the oven and cool for 2 minutes before transferring them to a wire rack to cool completely.

Coffee and Irish-Cream Dreams

Joanne Holtmeier of Edina anchored her recipe on the appeal of the liqueur known as Bailey's Irish Cream. "Do we even know what the flavor of Bailey's is?" she said. "I can't put my finger on just what exactly that flavor is, other than 'good.'" The recipe features a second key ingredient, and that's instant coffee. "Ina Garten always puts instant espresso powder into all of her chocolate baked goods, and now I do, too," said Holtmeier. "You can't really taste it, but it does make the chocolate taste better."

MAKES 3 DOZEN COOKIES

FOR COOKIES

2 1/2 cups flour

2 tablespoons instant coffee powder

1 1/2 teaspoons baking soda

3/4 teaspoon salt

1/2 teaspoon baking powder

1/2 cup (1 stick) unsalted butter, at room temperature

3/4 cup packed light brown sugar

3/4 cup granulated sugar

1 egg

1/2 cup Irish cream liqueur (such as Bailey's)

FOR GLAZE

2 cups powdered sugar

2 to 4 tablespoons Irish cream liqueur (such as Bailey's)

Brown and white decorative sprinkles, optional

NOTE This dough must be prepared in advance. For a less-boozy glaze, substitute milk or cream for half the amount of the Irish cream liqueur.

TO PREPARE COOKIES: In a medium bowl, whisk together the flour, instant coffee powder, baking soda, salt, and baking powder, and reserve.

In the bowl of an electric mixer on medium-high speed, beat the butter, brown sugar, and granulated sugar until light and fluffy, about 2 minutes. Add the egg and Irish cream liqueur and beat until thoroughly combined. Reduce the speed to low, add the flour mixture, and mix until just combined. Cover the bowl with plastic wrap and refrigerate for 30 minutes.

When ready to bake, preheat the oven to 350°F and line the baking sheets with parchment paper.

Shape the dough into 1-inch balls, and place 2 inches apart on the prepared baking sheets. Bake until the cookies are set and beginning to brown, about 10 to 13 minutes. Remove the cookies from the oven and cool for 2 minutes before transferring them to a wire rack to cool completely.

TO PREPARE GLAZE: Place a wire rack over wax paper or parchment paper. In a small bowl, whisk together the powdered sugar with 2 tablespoons of the Irish cream liqueur, adding more as needed, up to 2 additional tablespoons; the mixture should be thick enough to coat cookies. Frost each cookie with the glaze, and decorate with the brown and white sprinkles (optional). Allow the glaze to set before serving.

Cranberry Cat Kisses

Anne Park and her daughter Hannah Park, both of St. Paul, created this recipe while driving. Well, at least the idea for it. "We were talking about what makes a good holiday cookie," said Anne. "My contribution was chocolate." And Hannah? Cranberries. "I really like Craisins," she said, referring to dried cranberries. "Mom was convinced that cherries would be better, but I knew cranberries would be better." Back in their St. Paul kitchen, they borrowed ideas from other favorite cookies: the taste of butter from spritz, an egg-free formula from Russian tea cakes ("So we could bake without having any eggs in the house," said Anne), and a chocolate-dipped coating from peanut butter balls. Cat Kisses (a nod to the family feline, Neko) was an immediate hit. Just another day's work for this mother–daughter team.

MAKES 4 DOZEN COOKIES

FOR COOKIES

1 cup (2 sticks) unsalted butter, at room temperature
1/2 cup powdered sugar
1/2 teaspoon almond extract
2 1/4 cups flour
3/4 cup finely chopped almonds
1/2 cup dried cranberries, finely chopped

FOR CHOCOLATE COATING

1 cup semisweet chocolate chips
2 tablespoons shortening
Sliced almonds for decoration

TO PREPARE COOKIES: Preheat the oven to 400°F and line the baking sheets with parchment paper.

In the bowl of an electric mixer on medium-high speed, beat the butter until creamy, about 1 minute. Add the powdered sugar and beat until light and fluffy, about 2 minutes. Add the almond extract and beat until thoroughly combined. Reduce the speed to low, add the flour, and mix until just combined. Stir in the almonds and dried cranberries.

Shape the dough into 1-inch balls, and place 2 inches apart on the prepared baking sheets. Bake until the cookies are set but not browned, 7 to 8 minutes. Remove the cookies from the oven and cool for 5 minutes before transferring them to a wire rack to cool completely.

TO PREPARE CHOCOLATE COATING: In a double boiler over gently simmering water (or in a bowl in a microwave oven), combine the chocolate chips and shortening, whisking occasionally until smooth. Dip the top of the cookies in the melted chocolate and decorate with an almond slice. Transfer them to wax paper and allow the chocolate to set before serving.

Devil's Delight Cookies

Michelle Clark's minor obsession with a dark chocolate–chipotle truffle made by a St. Paul chocolatier got her thinking: could it translate into a cookie? The Minneapolis resident kicked the idea around for a while before formulating an unforgettable recipe. "This cookie has fun with your tongue," she said. "You take a bite and you get one flavor; then you chew and you get another flavor. It's not just a sugar cookie or your basic Santa cutout cookie, but it has both chocolate and cinnamon, and those are holiday flavors to me. Besides, to have the scent of chocolate and cinnamon in the oven, well, what's more Christmas than that?"

MAKES 2 DOZEN COOKIES

FOR DUSTING MIXTURE

4 teaspoons granulated sugar

4 teaspoons ground cinnamon

1/8 teaspoon cayenne pepper

FOR COOKIES

10 ounces bittersweet chocolate, chopped

1/2 cup plus 2 teaspoons flour

3 tablespoons unsweetened cocoa powder

1/4 teaspoon baking powder

1/4 teaspoon cayenne pepper

1/4 teaspoon salt

5 tablespoons unsalted butter, at room temperature

1 cup plus 1 tablespoon granulated sugar

3 eggs

2 teaspoons vanilla extract

3 ounces chocolate bar with cinnamon and red chile, chopped (see Note)

1/2 cup cinnamon chips

NOTE Two options for chile- and cinnamon-infused chocolate bars are Chuao Chocolatier's Spicy Maya and Lindt's Excellence Chili Dark Chocolate.

TO PREPARE DUSTING MIXTURE: In a small bowl, whisk together the granulated sugar, cinnamon, and cayenne pepper, and reserve.

TO PREPARE COOKIES: Preheat the oven to 350°F and line the baking sheets with parchment paper.

In a double boiler over gently simmering water (or in a bowl in a microwave oven), melt the bittersweet chocolate, whisking occasionally until smooth. Remove from the heat and cool for 10 minutes.

In a medium bowl, whisk together the flour, cocoa powder, baking powder, cayenne pepper, and salt, and reserve. In the bowl of an electric mixer on medium-high speed, beat the butter until creamy, about 1 minute. Add the granulated sugar and beat until light and fluffy, about 2 minutes. Add the eggs, one at a time, beating well after each addition. Continue to beat until the mixture is pale, light, and creamy, about 5 minutes. Reduce the speed to low, add the lukewarm melted chocolate and vanilla extract, and mix until just combined. Using a spatula, fold in the flour mixture, and then fold in the chopped cinnamon–chile chocolate bar and cinnamon chips.

Shape the dough into 1-inch balls, and place 2 inches apart on the prepared baking sheets. Sprinkle a pinch of the dusting mixture over each cookie, and bake until the tops are evenly cracked but the cookies are not yet firm to the touch, about 12 to 14 minutes. Remove the cookies from the oven and cool them completely on the baking sheets.

Diablo Snowballs

By borrowing elements from what were a specialty of her mother's formidable holiday baking regime, Becky Brandt of Long Lake honors cherished family traditions. At the same time, she inserts her own personality into the mix by adding cocoa powder, chocolate chips, and cayenne pepper. "They're a twist on a classic," she said. "I like them because I'm a chocolate lover, but they also remind me of my mom. I like to customize things. There are so many different versions of recipes, which means that you can take what you like from them and make them your own."

MAKES 3 DOZEN COOKIES

1 cup (2 sticks) unsalted butter, at room
   temperature
1 cup powdered sugar, divided
1/2 cup unsweetened cocoa powder, divided
1 teaspoon vanilla extract
1/4 teaspoon ground cayenne pepper
1 1/2 teaspoons ground cinnamon, divided
1/4 teaspoon salt
2 cups flour
1/2 cup chocolate chips
1/2 cup chopped toasted pecans (see Note)

NOTE To toast pecans, place the nuts in a dry skillet over medium heat and cook, stirring (or shaking the pan frequently), until they just begin to release their fragrance, about 3 to 4 minutes (alternatively, preheat the oven to 325°F, spread the nuts on an ungreased baking sheet and bake, stirring often, for 4 to 6 minutes).

Preheat the oven to 325°F and line the baking sheets with parchment paper.

In the bowl of an electric mixer on medium-high speed, beat the butter until creamy, about 1 minute. Reduce the speed to medium-low, add 1/2 cup powdered sugar, 1/4 cup cocoa powder, and vanilla extract, and mix until thoroughly combined. Reduce the speed to low, add the cayenne pepper, 1 teaspoon cinnamon, salt, and as much of the flour as your mixer can handle, mixing

until just combined. Stir in the remaining flour, then stir in the chocolate chips and pecans. Shape the dough into 1-inch balls, and place 2 inches apart on the prepared baking sheets. Bake for 19 minutes. Remove the cookies from the oven and cool for 2 minutes before transferring them to a wire rack to cool completely.

In a shallow bowl, combine the remaining 1/2 cup powdered sugar, the remaining 1/4 cup cocoa powder, and the remaining 1/2 teaspoon cinnamon. Roll the cookies in the cocoa-cinnamon mixture until coated.

Double-Chocolate Cherry Drops

Faith Ford of Big Lake has been making this brownie-like treat for what feels like forever. "It's a standard that I have to make, or people have a meltdown," she said with a laugh. "I bring them to work every year. People wait for them." The recipe's foundation was discovered in one of her grandmother's well-worn cookbooks, and the chocolate-with-cherry equation is rooted in another family connection. When Ford was a kid, her father would bring chocolate-covered cherries home every night between Thanksgiving and Christmas. He would give one to each of his children and then tell them if they found the box, they could eat the rest. "It wasn't until I was a teenager that I found out that he wasn't hiding them," Ford said with a laugh. "He was eating them."

MAKES 2 DOZEN COOKIES

1 tablespoon instant espresso powder
1 cup flour
3/4 cup unsweetened cocoa powder
1 teaspoon baking soda
1/4 teaspoon salt
1/2 cup (1 stick) unsalted butter, at room temperature
2/3 cup granulated sugar
1/4 cup packed dark brown sugar
1 egg
1/4 teaspoon vanilla extract
1/2 cup chopped dried cherries
3/4 cup semisweet chocolate chips
White chocolate for decoration, optional

Preheat the oven to 350°F and line the baking sheets with parchment paper.

In a small bowl, mix the espresso powder and 1 tablespoon boiling water, and reserve. In a small bowl, whisk together the flour, cocoa powder, baking soda, and salt, and reserve.

In the bowl of an electric mixer on medium-high speed, beat the butter until creamy, about 1 minute. Add the granulated sugar and beat until light and fluffy, about 2 minutes. Add the brown sugar and beat until thoroughly combined. Add the egg and beat until thoroughly combined. Add the vanilla extract and reserved espresso mixture, and beat until thoroughly combined. Reduce the speed to low, add the flour mixture, and mix until just combined. Stir in the cherries and chocolate chips.

Shape the dough into 1-inch balls, and place 2 inches apart on the prepared baking sheets. Bake for 8 to 10 minutes. Because the cookies are very dark, it's difficult to tell if they are overbaked. Watch the center of the cookies. When they lose their gooey quality, they are done. Remove the cookies from the oven and cool for 10 minutes before transferring them to a wire rack to cool completely.

If desired, in a double boiler over gently simmering water (or in a bowl in a microwave oven), melt the white chocolate, whisking occasionally until smooth. Drizzle the melted white chocolate over the cookies (optional).

Espresso Hazelnut Truffle Cookies

Why chocolate? That's easy. "My kids love chocolate," said Cheryl Francke of Arden Hills, who also observed that any chocolate dessert on her sprawling Thanksgiving buffet that includes the word "truffle" in its name always disappears quickly. "I have a chocolate-truffle torte and I thought, 'Maybe I could make a cookie that comes close to that,'" she said. Our judges were instantly smitten. "It's intense, in a good way," said one. "It's the grown-up version of that popular chocolate–peppermint cookie," said another. There was no hesitation when Francke was asked about the one baking tool she couldn't live without. "My mixer," she said. "I have a KitchenAid, and it's the greatest thing in the world. I don't think there is a week that goes by that I'm not using it. There's always something going on in that kitchen."

MAKES 3 DOZEN COOKIES

FOR COOKIES

4 ounces unsweetened chocolate

1 ¼ cup mini semisweet chocolate chips, divided

2 teaspoons instant espresso powder

⅓ cup (5 ⅓ tablespoons) unsalted butter, at room temperature

¾ cup flour

2 tablespoons unsweetened cocoa powder

¼ teaspoon baking powder

¼ teaspoon salt

1 cup granulated sugar

3 eggs

¼ cup finely chopped hazelnuts

FOR GLAZE

⅓ cup mini semisweet chocolate chips

1 tablespoon vegetable oil

¼ cup finely chopped hazelnuts

NOTE This dough must be prepared in advance.

TO PREPARE COOKIES: In a double boiler over gently simmering water (or in a bowl in a microwave oven), combine the unsweetened chocolate, 1 cup chocolate chips, espresso powder, and butter, whisking occasionally until smooth. Remove the chocolate mixture from the heat and cool for 10 minutes.

In a medium bowl, whisk together the flour, cocoa powder, baking powder, and salt, and reserve. In the bowl of an electric mixer on medium-high speed, beat the granulated sugar and eggs until light and airy, about 2 minutes. Add the chocolate mixture and beat until thoroughly combined. Reduce the speed to low, add the flour mixture, and mix until just combined. Stir in the remaining ¼ cup chocolate chips and the hazelnuts. Cover the bowl with plastic wrap and refrigerate for at least 6 hours, or overnight.

When ready to bake, preheat the oven to 350°F and line the baking sheets with parchment paper. Place a wire rack over wax paper or parchment paper.

Shape the dough into 1-inch balls, and place 2 inches apart on the prepared baking sheets, flattening the dough slightly. Bake until lightly puffed and just set, about 9 to 11 minutes. Remove the cookies from the oven and cool for 2 minutes before transferring them to a wire rack to cool completely.

TO PREPARE GLAZE: In a double boiler over gently simmering water (or in a bowl in a microwave oven), combine the chocolate chips and vegetable oil, whisking occasionally until smooth. Drizzle the melted chocolate over the cookies; sprinkle with the chopped hazelnuts. Allow the glaze to set before serving.

French–Swiss Butter Cookies

Years ago, Ramona Doebler of Elk River asked her mother to share a cherished recipe, a cinnamon-flavored sugar cookie. "But she couldn't find it," said Doebler. "So I sent a request into the newspaper," she said, referring to the then-new Taste section of the Minneapolis Star (now *Star Tribune)* and its instantly popular Readers' Exchange feature. Doebler still has the handwritten response, and the recipe. "I saw your request for cookies in today's paper," wrote Doebler's cookie guardian angel, otherwise known as Myrtle Eveland of Anoka. "I'm sure this is the one you want—so I'll send it directly to you. I hope you like them as well as I do."

MAKES 5 DOZEN COOKIES

1 cup (2 sticks) unsalted butter, at room
    temperature
1 cup granulated sugar
1 egg, separated
2 ½ teaspoons ground cinnamon
2 cups flour, plus extra for pressing dough
Finely chopped walnuts (or pecans or
    decorative sugar)

NOTE This dough must be prepared in advance.

In the bowl of an electric mixer on medium-high speed, beat the butter until creamy, about 1 minute. Gradually add the granulated sugar and beat until light and fluffy, about 2 minutes. Add the egg yolk and beat until thoroughly combined. Reduce the speed to low, add the cinnamon and flour, and mix until just combined. Cover the bowl with plastic wrap and refrigerate for at least 1 hour.

When ready to bake, preheat the oven to 350°F and line the baking sheets with parchment paper.

In a small bowl, slightly beat the reserved egg white with a fork. Shape the dough into 1-inch balls, and place 2 inches apart on the prepared baking sheets. Dip a flat-bottomed glass in flour and press the dough to 1/16- to 1/8-inch thickness, re-flouring the glass with each cookie.

Brush a little of the egg white in the center of each cookie; then sprinkle the center with chopped walnuts (or pecans or decorative sugar). Bake 10 to 12 minutes. Remove the cookies from the oven and cool for 2 minutes before transferring them to a wire rack to cool completely.

Frosted Cashew Cookies

Two entries for the same cookie in 2005: what are the odds? For both contestants, Frosted Cashew Cookies go way back. Anne Marie Draganowski of West St. Paul found these in her grandmother's recipe box. "You see a lot of Christmas cookies with pecans, almonds, and walnuts," she said, "but not cashews." Once she tried the recipe, she loved it. DeNae Shewmake of Burnsville discovered them in an old American Crystal Sugar recipe collection, one of several hundred cookbooks in her library. The kitchen is the center of her home, and Shewmake is always expanding her cooking and baking repertoire. "I want to create new traditions for my family," she said.

MAKES 3 DOZEN COOKIES

FOR COOKIES

2 cups flour

¾ teaspoon baking soda

¾ teaspoon baking powder

¼ teaspoon salt

½ cup (1 stick) unsalted butter, at room temperature

1 cup packed light brown sugar

1 egg

½ teaspoon vanilla extract

⅓ cup sour cream

1 cup chopped salted cashews

FOR BROWN BUTTER

½ cup (1 stick) unsalted butter

FOR ICING

3 tablespoons heavy cream

¼ teaspoon vanilla extract

2 to 2 ½ cups powdered sugar

Whole salted cashews

TO PREPARE COOKIES: Preheat the oven to 350°F and line the baking sheets with parchment paper.

In a medium bowl, whisk together the flour, baking soda, baking powder, and salt, and reserve.

In the bowl of an electric mixer on medium-high speed, beat the butter until creamy, about 1 minute. Add the brown sugar and beat until light and fluffy, about 2 minutes.

Add the egg and vanilla extract, and beat until thoroughly combined. Reduce the speed to low. Add the flour mixture in three additions, alternating with the sour cream and beginning and ending with the flour mixture. Mix until just combined. Fold in the chopped cashews.

Shape the dough into 1-inch balls, and place 2 inches apart on the prepared baking sheets. Bake until the cookies are just set and turning golden around the edges, about 10 to 12 minutes. Remove the cookies from the oven and cool for 2 minutes before transferring them to a wire rack to cool completely.

TO PREPARE BROWN BUTTER: In a medium saucepan over medium heat, melt the butter, stirring constantly, until the butter smells nutty and browned bits begin to form at the bottom of the pan, about 5 minutes. Remove from the heat.

TO PREPARE ICING: Add the cream and vanilla extract to the brown butter and whisk to combine. Add 1 ½ cups powdered sugar, whisking until smooth, gradually adding more powdered sugar, 1 tablespoon at a time, until the icing is thick enough to spread. Immediately ice the cookies and top each with a whole cashew. Allow the icing to set before serving.

Grasshoppers

Fans of the Girl Scouts' Thin Mints cookies will devour this soft, minty, chocolate-covered treat. For Joanne Holtmeier of Edina, her "Eureka" moment occurred while enjoying requisite Wisconsin supper club rituals during a visit to Creekside Supper Club in Minneapolis. "Those after-dinner drinks—Pink Squirrels, Golden Cadillacs, Grasshoppers—have 'cookie' written all over them," she said. Holtmeier, who often enlists the contents of her liquor cabinet in her baking, likes the symmetry of adding crème de menthe to a brownie-like cookie. "The flavor makes it more festive, fun, and holiday-ish," she said. Peppermint extract may be used instead of crème de menthe liqueur (see Note in recipe).

MAKES 3 DOZEN COOKIES

FOR COOKIES

½ cup (3 ounces) semisweet chocolate chips

1 ½ cups flour

¼ cup unsweetened cocoa powder

1 teaspoon baking powder

¼ teaspoon baking soda

¼ teaspoon salt

½ cup (1 stick) unsalted butter, at room temperature

⅓ cup granulated sugar

⅓ cup packed light brown sugar

1 egg

2 teaspoons crème de menthe liqueur (see Note)

⅓ cup buttermilk (see Note)

FOR FROSTING

6 tablespoons (¾ stick) unsalted butter

½ cup mint baking chips (see Note)

¼ cup milk

2 tablespoons unsweetened cocoa powder

2 teaspoons crème de menthe liqueur (see Note)

2 cups powdered sugar, divided

Mint baking chips or chopped Andes Chocolate Mints, optional (see Note)

NOTE This dough must be prepared in advance. Substitute peppermint extract for crème de menthe, if you prefer, using 1 ¼ teaspoons of peppermint extract for the dough and 1 teaspoon peppermint extract for the frosting. To make a buttermilk substitute, add 1 ½ teaspoons white vinegar to ½ cup milk. Andes Crème de Menthe baking chips are a widely available brand of mint baking chips. The dough is based on a recipe from thepioneerwoman.com.

TO PREPARE COOKIES: In a double boiler over gently simmering water (or in a bowl in a microwave oven), melt the chocolate chips, whisking occasionally until smooth. Remove from the heat and set aside to cool.

In a medium bowl, whisk together the flour, cocoa powder, baking powder, baking soda, and salt, and reserve.

In the bowl of an electric mixer on medium speed, beat the butter, granulated sugar, and brown sugar until light and fluffy, about 2 to 3 minutes. Add the egg, crème de menthe (or 1 ¼ teaspoons peppermint extract), and melted chocolate, and beat until thoroughly combined. Reduce the speed to low and add half of the flour mixture, mixing until just combined. Add the buttermilk, mixing just until combined, then add the remaining flour mixture, mixing until just combined. Cover the bowl with plastic wrap and refrigerate for 1 hour.

When ready to bake, preheat the oven to 350°F and line the baking sheets with parchment paper. Place a wire rack over wax paper or parchment paper.

Shape the dough into 1-inch balls, and place the cookies 2 inches apart on the prepared baking sheets. Bake until the tops of the cookies are puffed and the edges are set, about 8 to 10 minutes. Remove the cookies from the oven and cool for 5 minutes before transferring them to a wire rack to cool completely.

TO PREPARE FROSTING: In a medium saucepan over low heat, melt butter. Remove from the heat, add the mint baking chips and whisk until smooth. Add the milk, cocoa powder, crème de menthe (or 1 teaspoon peppermint extract), and whisk until smooth. Add 1 ½ cups powdered sugar and whisk until smooth, adding more powdered sugar, 1 tablespoon at a time (up to 8 tablespoons) to achieve the desired consistency. Generously spoon the frosting on the cookies, allowing it to drip down the sides. Sprinkle the mint baking chips (or chopped Andes Chocolate Mints) on the top of each cookie (optional). Allow the frosting to set before serving.

Hot and Sassy Peanut Butter Buds

Janet Heirigs of Minneapolis admitted that she's not much of a Christmas cookie baker, although she usually makes these spicy treats, along with cranberry biscotti and rum balls. This recipe began with good intentions, for a cookie. "When my kids were little, I was trying to feed them only wholesome things, and I found a recipe in Jane Brody's 1985 *Good Food* cookbook," she said. "It was called 'Peanut Butter Rounds,' and it was a boost of protein for my skinny little boys." All these years later, Heirigs has baked—and altered—the recipe so often "that it's never the same way twice," she said. That includes the inspired moment when she thought to add cayenne pepper. "Now they give you that nice, warm feeling," she said.

MAKES 3 DOZEN COOKIES

1 1/4 cups flour

1 teaspoon baking soda

1/2 teaspoon salt

1/4 teaspoon plus 1/8 teaspoon cayenne pepper, divided

1/4 teaspoon freshly ground nutmeg

2 tablespoons sesame seeds

1/2 cup crunchy peanut butter, at room temperature

1/3 cup (5 1/3 tablespoons) unsalted butter, at room temperature

1/2 cup packed light brown sugar

1 egg

1 teaspoon vanilla extract

1/4 cup granulated sugar

3 ounces dark chocolate bar infused with chile (see Note)

1/4 cup semisweet chocolate chips

3 ounces white chocolate

NOTE This dough must be prepared in advance. Two options for chile-infused chocolate bars are Chuao Chocolatier's Spicy Maya and Lindt's Excellence Chili Dark Chocolate.

In a medium bowl, whisk together the flour, baking soda, salt, 1/4 teaspoon cayenne pepper, nutmeg, and sesame seeds, and reserve.

In the bowl of an electric mixer on medium-high speed, beat the peanut butter and butter until creamy, about 1 minute. Add the brown sugar and beat until light and fluffy, about 2 minutes. Add the egg and vanilla extract, and beat until fully combined. Reduce the speed to low. Add the flour mixture in three additions, mixing until just combined. Cover the bowl with plastic wrap and refrigerate overnight, or up to 2 days.

When ready to bake, preheat the oven to 350°F and line the baking sheets with parchment paper.

In a shallow bowl, whisk together the granulated sugar and the remaining 1/8 teaspoon cayenne pepper. Shape the dough into 1-inch balls. Roll the cookies in the sugar–cayenne pepper mixture to coat and place 2 inches apart on the prepared baking sheets. Bake until slightly browned, 10 to 12 minutes. Remove the cookies from the oven and cool for 5 minutes before transferring them to a wire rack to cool completely.

In a double boiler over gently simmering water (or in a bowl in a microwave oven), melt the dark chocolate bar and chocolate chips, whisking occasionally until smooth. Dip the tops of cookies into the melted chocolate. Place the cookies on wax paper and allow the chocolate to set. In a double boiler over simmering water (or in a bowl in a microwave oven) melt the white chocolate, whisking occasionally until smooth. Drizzle the melted white chocolate over the cookies. Allow the white chocolate to set before serving.

Hot Cocoa Cookies

After Macy Hennen of Pierz discovered this recipe online (we tracked a version of it to rachaelraymag.com), Hot Cocoa Cookies quickly became a favorite at the Hennens' annual December cook- and bake-a-thon. "It's a fun recipe to make," Hennen said. "These cookies get everyone in the Christmas mood." One judge noted, "Kids would like to make these." Another added: "And eat these."

MAKES 2 TO 3 DOZEN COOKIES
1 ½ cups flour
¼ cup unsweetened cocoa powder
1 ½ teaspoons baking powder
¼ teaspoon salt
16 ounces semisweet chocolate, divided
½ cup (1 stick) unsalted butter
1 ¼ cups packed light brown sugar
3 eggs
1 ½ teaspoons vanilla extract
Marshmallows, mini or regular

NOTE This dough must be prepared in advance. Feel free to experiment with the type of chocolate in this intensely chocolaty cookie. While the recipe calls for semisweet, a mix of bittersweet (chopped and melted for the dough) and semisweet (for the pieces under the marshmallow) is also a delicious combination.

In a medium bowl, whisk together the flour, cocoa powder, baking powder, and salt, and reserve. Chop 12 ounces of semisweet chocolate into ½-inch pieces. In a double boiler over gently simmering water (or in a bowl in a microwave oven), melt the butter and chopped chocolate, whisking occasionally until smooth. Remove from the heat and cool for 15 minutes.

In the bowl of an electric mixer on medium speed, beat the brown sugar, eggs, and vanilla extract until smooth, about 2 minutes. Add the melted chocolate mixture and beat until just blended. Reduce the speed to low. Add the flour mixture in two additions, mixing until just combined. Cover the bowl with plastic wrap and refrigerate for at least 1 hour.

When ready to bake, preheat the oven to 325°F and line the baking sheets with parchment paper.

Place a wire rack over wax paper or parchment paper. Break the remaining 4 ounces of chocolate into small pieces, and cut marshmallows (if necessary) into a size suitable for the top of the cookie. Shape the dough into 1-inch balls, and place 2 inches apart on the prepared baking sheets, flattening the dough slightly. Bake until the tops of the cookies crack, about 12 minutes.

Remove the cookies from the oven and gently press a chocolate piece, then a marshmallow, into each cookie. Return them to the oven and bake until the marshmallows are just softened, about 4 minutes. Remove the cookies from the oven and cool for 5 minutes before transferring them to the prepared wire rack. Grate any remaining chocolate over the warm cookies as a garnish.

Italian Almond Cookies

During a college study-abroad year at the Università di Bologna, William Teresa of Minneapolis dated a fellow student. The couple would frequently visit her family in Cesena, a small city in Emilia–Romagna, where Teresa became immersed in the cooking lives of his girlfriend's parents and grandparents. "They were so lovely," he said. "It was wonderful to be in a place where food is so rooted in tradition and place, and to encounter something that has always been made by the same people, with little variation." One of the Italian grandmothers baked a chewy-crispy and out-rageously rich almond cookie, which the family enjoyed with espresso. Teresa was instantly smitten and perfected the formula when he returned home. "They're not like any other American cookie," he said. "Maybe that's why so many people ask me for the recipe."

MAKES 2 DOZEN COOKIES

1 egg white
2 1/4 cups almond flour
3/4 cups granulated sugar
Freshly grated zest from 1 large lemon
1/8 teaspoon honey
1 teaspoon almond extract
1 teaspoon vanilla extract
Powdered sugar, for coating

NOTE These cookies are best enjoyed the day they are baked, and also freeze very well.

Preheat the oven to 350°F and line the baking sheets with parchment paper.

In the bowl of an electric mixer fitted with a whisk attachment on medium-high speed, whip the egg white until it forms soft peaks.

In a medium bowl, whisk together the almond flour, granulated sugar, and lemon zest. Stir in the egg white, honey, almond extract, and vanilla extract, and knead into a ball of dough (the dough will be slightly sticky). Shape the dough into a log measuring about 1 inch in diameter, giving the log an oval shape (one with distinctive wider and narrower ends) so that the cut cookies will resemble an egg shape. Using a sharp knife, cut the log at 1/2-inch intervals and form the dough into egg-shaped cookies.

Fill a shallow bowl with powdered sugar. Roll the cookies in the powdered sugar, coating all sides and gently tapping off excess powdered sugar. Place the cookies 1 inch apart on the prepared baking sheets (cookies spread only slightly) and bake until only slightly browned with a cracked exterior, about 15 to 20 minutes. Remove the cookies from the oven and cool for 5 minutes before transferring them to a wire rack to cool completely.

Italian Cream Cake Cookies

Joanne Holtmeier of Edina enjoys converting the building blocks of other desserts into cookies. "It's fun to invent things," she said. A colleague once baked a three-tiered pecan and coconut cake, with cream cheese frosting. "The recipe was from an old church cookbook, and it was called 'Italian Cream Cake,'" said Holtmeier. "I'm Italian-American and had never heard of it—it's really more of a Southern cake. It's my husband's favorite, and I've baked it for his birthday ever since."

MAKES 3 DOZEN COOKIES

FOR COOKIES

2 1/2 cups flour
1/2 teaspoon baking soda
1/2 teaspoon salt
1/2 cup (1 stick) butter, at room temperature
1 cup granulated sugar
1 egg
2 teaspoons vanilla extract
1/2 cup buttermilk (see Note)
1 cup chopped pecans (see Note)
1 cup sweetened shredded coconut

FOR GLAZE

1 1/2 cups powdered sugar
1 1/2 tablespoons cream cheese, at room temperature
1 1/2 tablespoons heavy cream or milk
3/4 teaspoon vanilla extract
About 36 whole pecans, for garnish (see Note)

NOTE To make a buttermilk substitute, add 1 1/2 teaspoons white vinegar to 1/2 cup milk. For added flavor, toast the pecans: place the nuts in a dry skillet over medium heat and cook, stirring (or shaking the pan frequently), until they just begin to release their fragrance, about 3 to 4 minutes (alternatively, preheat the oven to 325°F, spread the nuts on an ungreased baking sheet and bake, stirring often, for 4 to 6 minutes).

TO PREPARE COOKIES: Preheat the oven to 350°F and line the baking sheets with parchment paper. Place a wire rack over wax paper or parchment paper.

In a medium bowl, whisk together the flour, baking soda, and salt, and reserve.

In the bowl of an electric mixer on medium-high speed, beat the butter and granulated sugar until light and fluffy, about 2 minutes. Add the egg and vanilla extract and beat until thoroughly combined. Reduce the speed to low. Add the flour mixture in two additions, alternating with the buttermilk. Mix until just combined. Stir in the chopped pecans and coconut.

Shape the dough into 1-inch balls, and place 2 inches apart on the prepared baking sheets. Bake until the tops are barely set and are beginning to brown around the edges, about 13 minutes (because they are cakey cookies, do not underbake). Remove the cookies from the oven and cool for 2 minutes before transferring them to a wire rack to cool completely.

TO PREPARE GLAZE: In a medium bowl, whisk together the powdered sugar, cream cheese, cream (or milk), and vanilla extract, adjusting with the cream (or milk) to achieve the desired consistency. Allow the glaze to rest a few minutes before icing the cookies, as it will thicken slightly.

TO ASSEMBLE COOKIES: Spread glaze across the top of each cookie, then decorate the tops with a single pecan. Allow the glaze to set before serving.

Lime Coolers

One day at the supermarket, Stacy McNabb of Richfield spied a lime cookie recipe in a cooking magazine. She was intrigued and gave it a shot. Talk about a runaway hit. "If I put it on a tray, it's the one recipe that everyone wants—every time," she said. There's plenty to this cookie's curb appeal: tart citrus, a festive green tint, and a light bite. "I don't like those heavily chocolate, super-sweet cookies," McNabb said. "There are already so many of those."

MAKES 2 DOZEN COOKIES

FOR COOKIES

1 cup (2 sticks) unsalted butter, at room temperature, plus extra for flattening dough

1/2 cup powdered sugar

1 3/4 cups flour

1/4 cup cornstarch

1 tablespoon freshly grated lime zest, finely chopped

1/2 teaspoon vanilla extract

Granulated sugar for pressing dough

FOR LIME GLAZE

1/2 cup powdered sugar

2 to 3 teaspoons freshly grated lime zest, finely chopped

4 teaspoons freshly squeezed lime juice

NOTE This dough must be prepared in advance.

TO PREPARE COOKIES: In the bowl of an electric mixer on medium-high speed, beat the butter until creamy, about 1 minute. Add the powdered sugar and beat until light and fluffy, about 2 minutes. Reduce the speed to low, add the flour, cornstarch, lime zest, and vanilla extract, and mix until just combined. Cover the bowl with plastic wrap and refrigerate for at least 1 hour.

When ready to bake, preheat the oven to 350°F and line the baking sheets with parchment paper.

Place the granulated sugar into a shallow bowl. Shape the dough into 1-inch balls, and place about 2 inches apart on the prepared baking sheets. Spread a light coating of butter on the flat bottom of a glass, dip it into the granulated sugar, and carefully press the prepared glass bottom into a cookie, flattening it until the dough is about 1/4-inch thick; repeat with the remaining cookies. Bake until the edges are light golden brown, 9 to 11 minutes. Remove the cookies from the oven and cool for 2 minutes before transferring them to a wire rack to cool completely.

TO PREPARE LIME GLAZE: In a small bowl, whisk together the powdered sugar, lime zest, and lime juice, until a light glaze forms. Spread the glaze over the cookies. Allow the glaze to set before serving.

Limoncello Kisses

For Joanne Holtmeier of Edina, adding lemon to her go-to sugar cookie recipe from *Everyday Food* magazine was a no-brainer. "Everything citrus is my favorite," she said. "It balances out the sweetness of other holiday flavors." Dialing up the flavor with limoncello was inspired by her penchant for throwing cocktail parties. "I've purchased many liquors and liqueurs, and wondered how I could incorporate them into my baking. I love baking cookies. That's my hobby. Cookies make people happy."

MAKES 4 DOZEN COOKIES

FOR COOKIES

2 cups flour

1 teaspoon baking powder

1/2 teaspoon salt

1/4 teaspoon baking soda

1 1/2 cup granulated sugar

1 tablespoon freshly grated lemon zest

1/2 cup (1 stick) unsalted butter, at room temperature

1 egg

1 teaspoon vanilla extract

1 tablespoon freshly squeezed lemon juice

1/4 cup sour cream

FOR FROSTING

2 cups powdered sugar, plus extra if needed

3 tablespoons limoncello (see Note), plus extra if needed

1 tablespoon freshly squeezed lemon juice, plus extra if needed

Candied lemon slices

Freshly grated lemon zest, or decorative sprinkles, optional

NOTE Limoncello is an Italian lemon liqueur. If you don't want to use an alcoholic beverage as an ingredient, substitute cream or milk in the frosting (do not substitute lemon juice, as it will be too tart).

TO PREPARE COOKIES: Preheat the oven to 350°F and line the baking sheets with parchment paper.

In a medium bowl, whisk together the flour, baking powder, salt, and baking soda, and reserve.

In a medium bowl, combine the granulated sugar and lemon zest. Using your fingers, rub the zest into the sugar until fragrant, about 30 seconds.

In the bowl of an electric mixer on medium-high speed, beat the butter until creamy, about 1 minute. Add the lemon sugar and beat until light and fluffy, about 2 minutes. Add the egg, vanilla extract, and lemon juice, and beat until thoroughly combined. Reduce the speed to low. Add the flour mixture in two additions, alternating with the sour cream. Mix until just combined.

Shape the dough into 1-inch balls, and place 2 inches apart on the prepared baking sheets. Bake until the cookies are just firm and the tops are barely beginning to brown, about 10 to 12 minutes. Remove the cookies from the oven and cool for 2 minutes before transferring them to a wire rack to cool completely.

TO PREPARE FROSTING: In a medium bowl, whisk together the powdered sugar, limoncello, and lemon juice. Add more powdered sugar or lemon juice, as necessary, to achieve the desired consistency. Frost the top of each cookie (or drizzle the frosting over it) and top each cookie with a candied lemon slice. Add the lemon zest, or sprinkles (optional). Allow the frosting to set before serving.

Malted Milk Ball Cookies

Micah Zupke of Lakeville taught herself to bake by watching YouTube how-to videos. By the time she was in ninth grade, she was operating a baking business, selling cookies, cakes, and cupcakes through a website. These festive cookies grew out of a recipe exchange, with Zupke (who was a college senior when she entered the contest) making key ingredient substitutions out of dietary necessity. "There aren't many candies I can eat because of my peanut allergy," she said. "But I'm 100 percent a malted milk ball fan."

MAKES 3 DOZEN COOKIES

FOR COOKIES

2 cups flour

2/3 cup malted milk powder (see Note)

1 teaspoon baking soda

1 teaspoon salt

3/4 cup (1 1/2 sticks) unsalted butter, at room temperature

1/4 cup shortening

3/4 cup packed light brown sugar

1 tablespoon vanilla extract

1 egg

1 egg yolk

FOR BROWN BUTTER

3/4 cup (1 1/2 sticks) unsalted butter

FOR FROSTING

4 cups powdered sugar, plus more as needed

1 cup malted milk powder (see Note)

1/2 teaspoon salt

2 teaspoons vanilla extract

1/2 cup heavy cream, plus more as needed

Malted milk balls, whole or chopped, for garnish

NOTE This dough must be prepared in advance. Plain malted milk powder or chocolate-flavored malted milk powder are equally suitable in this cookie. The malted milk powder may need to be sifted to remove lumps before adding it to the recipe. For those who prefer sandwich-style cookies, consider following that format.

TO PREPARE COOKIES: In a medium bowl, whisk together the flour, malted milk powder, baking soda, and 1 teaspoon salt, and reserve.

In the bowl of an electric mixer on medium-high speed, beat the butter, shortening, brown sugar, and vanilla extract until light and fluffy, about 2 minutes. Add the egg and egg yolk and beat until fully combined. Reduce the speed to low, add the flour mixture, and mix until just a few streaks of flour remain. Continue to stir by hand to combine. Form the dough into a disk, wrap in plastic wrap, and refrigerate for at least 1 hour, or up to 24 hours.

When ready to bake, preheat the oven to 350°F and line the baking sheets with parchment paper.

Shape the dough into 1-inch balls, and place 2 inches apart on the prepared baking sheets. Bake until the tops of the cookies are lightly browned, about 10 to 12 minutes. Remove the cookies from the oven and cool for 2 minutes before transferring them to a wire rack to cool completely.

TO PREPARE BROWN BUTTER: In a medium saucepan over medium heat, melt the butter, stirring constantly, until the butter smells nutty and browned bits begin to form at the bottom of the pan, about 5 minutes. Remove from the heat, transfer the brown butter to a small bowl and cool slightly.

TO PREPARE FROSTING: In the bowl of an electric mixer on low speed, combine the powdered sugar, malted milk powder, salt, cooled brown butter, vanilla extract, and heavy cream, and mix until combined. Increase the speed to medium and mix until the frosting is smooth and creamy, adjusting with powdered sugar or cream to achieve the desired consistency.

TO ASSEMBLE COOKIES: Transfer the frosting into a piping bag (alternately, transfer frosting to a plastic bag, and cut out the corner) and pipe a frosting circle on the top of each cookie. Garnish with a whole malted milk ball, or with chopped malted milk balls.

Maple-Roasted Walnut Delights

Although maple-roasted walnuts are the irresistible centerpiece of this appealing cookie, another key ingredient is sumac. "While I was reading about sumac, I learned that it was a way to add brightness, acidity, and sourness to things," said Stephanie Steinwedel of Minneapolis. "That made me wonder how it would work in baked goods." The recipe yields more maple-roasted walnuts than a batch of cookies require. Thank goodness, because the delicious leftovers can be put to all kinds of uses: treat them as a snack, serve them in salads or on a cheese tray, or package them for gifts.

MAKES 3 DOZEN COOKIES

FOR MAPLE-ROASTED WALNUTS

1 pound walnuts

1/3 cup maple syrup

2 tablespoons olive oil

1/4 cup white sesame seeds

1/4 teaspoon ground cayenne red pepper, optional (see Note)

1/2 teaspoon freshly ground black pepper

1 teaspoon kosher salt, divided

1 tablespoon ground sumac (see Note)

FOR COOKIES

2 1/4 cups flour

3/4 teaspoon baking powder

1/2 teaspoon plus 1/8 teaspoon baking soda

1/4 teaspoon salt

10 tablespoons (1 stick plus 2 tablespoons) unsalted butter, at room temperature

2/3 cup packed light brown sugar

1/2 cup granulated sugar

1 egg

1 teaspoon vanilla extract

NOTE This dough must be prepared in advance. Ground sumac is available in the bulk spices section of most natural foods co-ops and online. For those who don't like heat in their cookies, skip the cayenne red pepper. Or try ancho chile powder, which is made with dried poblano peppers and delivers a slightly smoky flavor with less heat. The dough is inspired by a recipe from thedreameryevents.com, and the roasted walnuts formula is based on a recipe from cookinglight.com.

TO PREPARE MAPLE-ROASTED WALNUTS: Preheat the oven to 325°F. Place the walnuts in a large bowl, breaking up the walnuts slightly into smaller pieces with your hands. Drizzle with the maple syrup and olive oil, and sprinkle the sesame seeds, cayenne red pepper (optional), black pepper, and 1/2 teaspoon kosher salt. Toss until evenly coated. Spread the walnuts in a single layer on a rimmed baking sheet and roast, stirring occasionally, until the walnuts are golden brown and the maple syrup is caramelized, about 15 minutes. Remove the walnuts from the oven and immediately sprinkle with the sumac and remaining 1/2 teaspoon kosher salt. Cool completely. You will have extra maple-roasted walnuts; store them in an airtight container.

TO PREPARE COOKIES: Preheat the oven to 350°F and line the baking sheets with parchment paper.

In a medium bowl, whisk together the flour, baking powder, baking soda, and salt, and reserve.

In the bowl of an electric mixer on medium-high speed, beat the butter, brown sugar, and granulated sugar until light and fluffy, about 2 to 3 minutes. Add the egg and vanilla extract, and beat until thoroughly combined. Reduce the speed to low, add the flour mixture, and mix until just combined. Chop approximately 1 cup of the maple-roasted walnuts and fold them into the dough. Shape the dough into 1-inch balls, and place 2 inches apart on the prepared baking sheets. Lightly press a piece (or several pieces) of maple-roasted walnuts into the top of each cookie. Bake until golden brown, about 8 to 10 minutes. Remove the cookies from the oven and cool for 5 minutes before transferring them to a wire rack to cool completely.

Mocha Cappuccino Cookies

"Every Christmas, I try to invent a new cookie," said Joan Hause of Lake Elmo. "I am the auntie who brings the platter full of goodies—the fudge, the spritz, the sugar cookie, along with a new creation." That drive to innovate was tapped as she was enjoying a cappuccino. "I looked at the swirly top and started thinking that it might be kind of pretty in a cookie," she said. "I've never made a cookie with coffee in it before. And I do like frosting." Our judges do, too. "This is the first cookie that anyone would reach for on a cookie platter," said one. "Look how pretty this is," added another.

MAKES 4 DOZEN COOKIES

FOR COOKIES

2/3 cup unsweetened cocoa powder

1/2 teaspoon salt

2 teaspoons instant espresso powder

2 cups flour

1 cup (2 sticks) unsalted butter, at room temperature

1 1/3 cups granulated sugar

2 egg yolks

1/4 cup milk

2 teaspoons vanilla extract

FOR FROSTINGS

3 ounces white chocolate

3 ounces bittersweet chocolate

1/2 cup (1 stick) unsalted butter, at room temperature

1 1/4 cups powdered sugar

1 teaspoon vanilla extract

NOTE This cookie has two types of frosting for added effect.

TO PREPARE COOKIES: Preheat the oven to 350°F and line the baking sheets with parchment paper.

In a medium bowl, whisk together the cocoa powder, salt, espresso powder, and flour, and reserve.

In the bowl of an electric mixer on medium-high speed, beat the butter until creamy, about 1 minute. Add the granulated sugar and beat until light and fluffy, about 2 minutes. Add the egg yolks, milk, and vanilla extract, and beat until thoroughly combined. Reduce the speed to low, add the flour mixture, and mix until just combined.

Shape the dough into 1 1/2-inch balls and place 2 inches apart on the prepared baking sheets. Using a wide-bottomed glass, carefully press the dough to 1/2-inch thickness before baking. Bake until the cookies are set and the tops are dry, about 8 to 9 minutes. Remove the cookies from the oven and cool for 2 minutes before transferring them to a wire rack to cool completely.

TO PREPARE FROSTINGS: In a double boiler over gently simmering water (or in a bowl in a microwave oven), melt the white chocolate, whisking occasionally until smooth. Remove from the heat. Using the same method, melt the bittersweet chocolate, whisking occasionally until smooth. Remove from the heat. Allow the melted white chocolate and the melted bittersweet chocolate to cool slightly.

In the bowl of an electric mixer on medium-high speed, beat the butter until creamy, about 1 minute. Reduce the speed to medium-low and add the powdered sugar and vanilla extract, and mix until creamy, about 2 minutes. Divide the frosting

into two equal portions and place in separate medium bowls. Add the melted white chocolate to one bowl and the melted bittersweet chocolate to the other, stirring until thoroughly combined. If either frosting needs to be thicker, add more powdered sugar.

Create a white chocolate / bittersweet chocolate swirl on top of each cookie, about 2 teaspoons per cookie; a medium-size star tip works well. If using a pastry bag, use a coupler that allows you to attach 2 pastry bags, one for each frosting. The same effect can be made by placing 1 teaspoon of each icing on top of a cookie and swirling the frosting with a butter knife.

Nut Goodie Thumbprints

Crystal Schlueter of Babbitt is nutty about Nut Goodies: "I've always been a fan," she said. "In the checkout line at the grocery store, Mom would let me buy a candy bar, and it was always the one I'd choose. Of course, it's a Minnesota classic." It sure is: Pearson's Candy Company in St. Paul has been producing the chocolate–maple–peanut confection since 1912. For her candy bar–inspired recipe, Schlueter deviated slightly from the original, replacing milk chocolate with semisweet. Another alteration from Pearson's formula is the inclusion of salted peanuts. "I like the fact that the cookie is chewy and crispy, and that very sweet maple filling is different from the crunchy, salty peanuts," said Schlueter. "That's a combination a lot of people like."

MAKES 2 DOZEN COOKIES

FOR COOKIES

1 cup flour

1/3 cup unsweetened cocoa powder

1/4 teaspoon salt

1/2 cup (1 stick) unsalted butter, at room temperature

2/3 cup packed light brown sugar

1 egg, separated

2 tablespoons whole milk

2 teaspoons vanilla extract

3/4 cup chopped roasted and salted peanuts

FOR FILLING

2 tablespoons unsalted butter, at room temperature

2 tablespoons sweetened condensed milk

1 teaspoon maple extract

1/2 teaspoon vanilla extract

1 1/2 teaspoons whole milk

1 cup powdered sugar

FOR GANACHE

1/2 cup semisweet chocolate chips

2 tablespoons heavy cream

NOTE This dough must be prepared in advance.

TO PREPARE COOKIES: In a medium bowl, whisk together the flour, cocoa powder, and salt, and reserve. In the bowl of an electric mixer on medium-high speed, beat together the butter and brown sugar until light and fluffy, about 2 minutes. Add the egg yolk, milk, and vanilla extract, and beat until thoroughly combined. Reduce the speed to low, add the flour mixture, and mix until just combined. Form the dough into a disk, wrap in plastic wrap, and refrigerate for at least 30 minutes.

When ready to bake, preheat the oven to 350°F and line the baking sheets with parchment paper. Place a wire rack over wax paper or parchment paper.

Shape the dough into 1-inch balls. Dip the top half of each cookie into the reserved egg white and then into the peanuts. Place the cookies, peanut-side up, 2 inches apart on the prepared baking sheets. Using the back of a spoon or your thumb, press an indentation into the center of each cookie. Bake until the cookies are set but still soft, about 10 to 12 minutes. Remove the cookies from the oven and carefully remake the same slight indentation into the top of each cookie. Cool the cookies for 5 minutes before transferring them to a wire rack to cool completely.

TO PREPARE FILLING: In the bowl of an electric mixer on medium speed, combine the butter, condensed milk, maple extract, vanilla extract, whole milk, and powdered sugar. Beat until uniform and creamy.

While the cookies are still slightly warm, spoon the filling into the indentation in the cookies; then allow them to cool completely.

TO PREPARE GANACHE: In a double boiler over gently simmering water (or in a bowl in a microwave oven), combine the chocolate and cream, whisking occasionally until smooth. Drizzle the ganache over the cookies. Allow the ganache to set before serving.

Orange Almond Melting Moments

While conducting research on Swedish immigrant food traditions, Patrice Johnson of Roseville was told by an elderly woman that she had to try the cookie called Melting Moments. "I learned that these cookies used to be as popular as chocolate chip cookies are today," said Johnson. One slight hitch, however: "I haven't found any evidence that it's a Scandinavian cookie," she said with a laugh. "But I love that it's so simple, just five ingredients—and you always have them on hand—and some kind of flavoring." After tinkering with the recipe, she decided to enter a lemon–basil variation in the Minnesota State Fair's baking competition. The humid weather had other ideas, and Johnson went back to the drawing board, this time looking back on the Danish pastries her mother baked on Christmas morning. Bingo.

MAKES 2 DOZEN COOKIES

FOR COOKIES

1 cup flour

2/3 cup cornstarch

1/4 teaspoon ground cayenne pepper

1/4 teaspoon salt

1 cup (2 sticks) unsalted butter, cut into
  tablespoons, at room temperature

1/3 cup powdered sugar

Freshly grated zest from 1 orange

1/2 teaspoon almond extract

FOR ICING

3 tablespoons freshly squeezed orange juice

1 tablespoon unsalted butter, at room
  temperature

1 teaspoon almond extract

1 teaspoon vanilla extract

1/4 teaspoon salt

2 3/4 cups powdered sugar

1/2 cup raw sliced almonds for garnish

Freshly grated orange zest for garnish,
  optional

NOTE This dough must be prepared in advance.

TO PREPARE COOKIES: In a medium bowl, whisk together the flour, cornstarch, cayenne pepper, and salt, and reserve. In the bowl of an electric mixer on medium-high speed, beat the butter until creamy, about 1 minute. Add the powdered sugar, orange zest, and almond extract, and beat until light and fluffy, about 2 minutes. Reduce the speed to low, add the flour mixture, and mix until a grainy dough forms. Use your hands to form the dough into a round ball. Wrap the dough in plastic wrap and refrigerate for 30 to 60 minutes.

When ready to bake, preheat the oven to 325°F and line the baking sheets with parchment paper.

Shape the dough into 1-inch balls, and place 2 inches apart on the prepared baking sheets. Bake until the tops of the cookies are light in color, about 12 to 14 minutes. Remove the cookies from the oven and cool for 5 minutes before transferring them to a wire rack to cool completely.

TO PREPARE ICING: In the bowl of an electric mixer on medium speed, beat the orange juice, butter, almond extract, vanilla extract,

and salt until creamy, about 1 minute.
Reduce the speed to low, add the powdered
sugar, and mix until smooth. Using a small
spatula or knife (or a pastry bag), ice the
cookies. For a less sweet cookie, use only
1 teaspoon icing per cookie; for a sweeter
cookie, frost liberally with the icing. Garnish
with the almonds. Add the orange zest
(optional).

Orange Ginger Drops

"I associate the taste of ginger with this time of year," said Cheryl Francke of Arden Hills. "Whether it's gingerbread or gingersnaps, it's very reminiscent of the holidays. I've always had at least one ginger cookie combined into my holiday baking." She's constantly baking ("After a full day's work, you'll find me in the kitchen," she said) and twisting familiar flavors. "I thought I would experiment with crystallized ginger and see what I could come up with. Then I thought that orange would be a nice complement," she said. "It's good to know that playing in the kitchen pays off once in a while." That crystallized ginger–orange garnish is there for more than just flavor. "I think things taste better if they look better," she said. "I bake a lot of muffins, and I always like to top them with something, so when you look at them you know what you're biting into."

MAKES 4 DOZEN COOKIES

2 ¼ cups flour

2 teaspoons baking soda

¼ teaspoon salt

½ teaspoon ground cloves

1 teaspoon ground cinnamon

1 teaspoon ground ginger

1 tablespoon plus 2 teaspoons freshly grated orange zest, divided

1 tablespoon chopped crystallized ginger, plus extra for garnish

¾ cup (1 ½ sticks) unsalted butter, at room temperature

1 cup packed light brown sugar

1 egg

¼ cup molasses

1 tablespoon freshly squeezed orange juice

3 tablespoons granulated sugar

NOTE This dough must be prepared in advance.

In a medium bowl, whisk together the flour, baking soda, salt, cloves, cinnamon, ground ginger, 1 tablespoon orange zest, and crystallized ginger, and reserve. In the bowl of an electric mixer on medium-high speed, beat the butter and brown sugar until creamy, about 2 minutes. Add the egg, molasses, and orange juice, and beat until thoroughly combined. Reduce the speed to low, add the flour mixture, and mix until just combined. Cover the bowl with plastic wrap and refrigerate for at least 1 hour.

Meanwhile, in a small bowl, combine the remaining 2 teaspoons orange zest with the granulated sugar. Using your fingers, blend the mixture thoroughly until the orange zest has a crystallized appearance and texture, and reserve.

When ready to bake, preheat the oven to 375°F and line the baking sheets with parchment paper.

Shape the dough into 1-inch balls. Dip the cookies in the orange zest mixture and place, sugar-side up, 2 inches apart on the prepared baking sheets. Press a few pieces of the crystallized ginger into the sugared top. Bake until the cookies are set but not hard, 10 to 12 minutes. Remove the cookies from the oven and cool for 2 minutes before transferring them to a wire rack to cool completely.

Orange Kisses

Bette Revoir of St. Paul bakes every week—cakes are a particular favorite—but it is the cookies she calls "sweet as a kiss" that have helped create her winning baking reputation. She's baked them for everyone, from members of the nearby police precinct and former St. Paul mayor Randy Kelly to her large (and cookie-enthusiastic) family. "When my kids were little, they would sit around the kitchen table while I was baking," she said. "I'd give them the rejects. My husband likes to lick the frosting bowl."

MAKES 4 DOZEN COOKIES

FOR COOKIES

2 cups flour

1/2 teaspoon baking soda

1/2 teaspoon salt

1/2 teaspoon baking powder

2/3 cup (1 stick plus 2 2/3 tablespoons) unsalted butter, at room temperature

3/4 cup granulated sugar

1 egg

2 tablespoons freshly grated orange zest

1/2 cup freshly squeezed orange juice

FOR ICING

2 cups powdered sugar

2 tablespoons unsalted butter, at room temperature

2 tablespoons freshly squeezed orange juice, plus extra if needed

1 tablespoon freshly grated orange zest

NOTE This dough must be prepared in advance. You can also try other citrus, such as lemons.

TO PREPARE COOKIES: In a medium bowl, whisk together the flour, baking soda, salt, and baking powder, and reserve.

In the bowl of an electric mixer on medium-high speed, beat the butter until creamy, about 1 minute. Add the granulated sugar and beat until light and fluffy, about 2 minutes. Add the egg and beat until thoroughly combined. Add the orange zest and beat until thoroughly combined. Add the orange juice and beat for 30 seconds.

Reduce the speed to low, add the flour mixture, and mix until just combined. Cover the bowl with plastic wrap and refrigerate for at least 30 minutes.

When ready to bake, preheat the oven to 350°F and line the baking sheets with parchment paper.

Shape the dough into 1-inch balls, and place 2 inches apart on the prepared baking sheets. Bake until the edges of the cookies are lightly browned, about 8 to 10 minutes. Remove the cookies from the oven and cool for 5 minutes before transferring them to a wire rack to cool completely.

TO PREPARE ICING: In the bowl of an electric mixer on low speed, mix the powdered sugar, butter, orange juice, and orange zest until combined, adding more orange juice if necessary to achieve the desired consistency. Ice cookies to taste.

Persian Molasses Crinkles

A trip to Turkey proved inspirational for Lance Swanson of North Branch. "I fell in love with some of the flavors over there, and when I came home I started trying to re-create them," he said. "I saw the bottle of pomegranate molasses that was just sitting on our shelf and I thought, 'Why not replace regular molasses with it?' After a lot of trial and error, the results really brought me back to Turkey." Swanson is pleased with how easy these cookies are to prepare. "You mix, you scoop, you bake," he said. "That's it."

MAKES 3 DOZEN COOKIES

2 1/2 cups flour

2 teaspoons baking soda

1/4 teaspoon salt

3/4 cup butter

1 cup granulated sugar

6 tablespoons pomegranate molasses (see Note)

2 teaspoons freshly grated lemon zest

1 egg

3/4 cup slivered almonds, toasted and very finely chopped (see Note)

NOTE Find pomegranate molasses in Middle Eastern specialty stores or in the imported foods section of most supermarkets. To make your own, combine 4 cups pomegranate juice, 1/2 cup granulated sugar, and 1 tablespoon freshly squeezed lemon juice in a medium saucepan; cook over medium heat, stirring, until the granulated sugar dissolves. Reduce the heat to medium-low and cook until the mixture reduces to 1 cup and is the consistency of thick syrup, about 75 minutes. Remove the pan from the heat, cool for 30 minutes, and transfer to an uncovered glass jar to cool completely. To toast slivered almonds, place the nuts in a dry skillet over medium heat and cook, stirring or shaking the pan frequently, until they just begin to release their fragrance, about 3 to 4 minutes (alternately, preheat the oven to 325°F, spread the nuts on an ungreased baking sheet, and bake, stirring often, for 4 to 6 minutes). Remove the nuts from the heat and cool to room temperature. For best results with this recipe, beat the butter and sugar for a long time.

Preheat the oven to 350°F and line the baking sheets with parchment paper.

In a medium bowl, whisk together the flour, baking soda, and salt, and reserve.

In the bowl of an electric mixer on medium-high speed, beat the butter and granulated sugar until light and fluffy, about 2 minutes. Add the pomegranate molasses and lemon zest, and beat until thoroughly combined. Add the egg and beat until thoroughly combined. Reduce the speed to low, add the flour mixture, and mix until just combined (the dough will be soft).

Shape the dough into 1-inch balls. Dip the cookies into the chopped almonds and place 2 inches apart on the prepared baking sheets, almond-side up. Bake until the cookies are puffed and deeply cracked, 10 to 12 minutes. Remove the cookies from the oven and cool for 2 minutes before transferring them to a wire rack to cool completely.

Pumpkin Cookies

For as long as she can remember, Amy Karlen of Minnetonka has been crazy about the Pumpkin Cookies that her mother, Judy, makes. "For years, I've been telling Mom that this is the best cookie, that it would win contests," she said. "But I know she would never think anything she made would ever be that good." Karlen has spent a considerable amount of time turning her friends and colleagues into Pumpkin Cookie converts, too. "So many people say, 'I don't like pumpkin,' but then they like these cookies," said Karlen. "They're cakey and sweet and spicy. They have always reminded me of autumn."

MAKES 3 DOZEN COOKIES

FOR COOKIES

3 1/2 cups flour

2 teaspoons baking soda

1 teaspoon salt

2 teaspoons ground cinnamon

1 1/2 teaspoons freshly grated nutmeg

1 teaspoon ground ginger

1/2 teaspoon ground cloves

1 cup shortening

2 cups granulated sugar

2 eggs, beaten

1 cup pumpkin purée (see Note)

FOR ICING

5 tablespoons light brown sugar

3 tablespoons unsalted butter

5 tablespoons milk

1 cup powdered sugar, plus extra if needed

NOTE Be sure to use canned pumpkin purée and not canned pumpkin pie filling.

TO PREPARE COOKIES: Preheat the oven to 350°F and line the baking sheets with parchment paper.

In a medium bowl, whisk together the flour, baking soda, salt, cinnamon, nutmeg, ginger, and cloves, and reserve.

In the bowl of an electric mixer on medium-high speed, beat the shortening and granulated sugar until creamy, about 2 minutes. Add the eggs, one at a time,

beating well after each addition. Add the pumpkin purée and beat until thoroughly combined. Reduce the speed to low, add the flour mixture, and mix until just combined.

Shape the dough into 1-inch balls, and place 2 inches apart on the prepared baking sheets. Bake for 10 minutes. Remove the cookies from the oven and cool for 5 minutes before transferring them to a wire rack to cool completely.

TO PREPARE ICING: In a small saucepan over medium heat, combine the brown sugar, butter, and milk, and bring the mixture to a boil. Remove from the heat, set aside, and cool completely, about an hour. Add the powdered sugar and whisk until the icing is the desired consistency, adding more if necessary. Ice cookies to taste. Allow the icing to set before serving.

Ricotta Sugar Cookies

Mary Beth Conzett of Plymouth was thumbing through *Good Housekeeping* magazine when she happened on this recipe. "I'm always looking for something different, and I love Italian food," Conzett said. "These were calling my name." It's difficult to imagine a more tender sugar cookie, and they come together in a snap. "They're so easy to make that it's almost embarrassing," she said. Turns out, it was already a winning recipe. Conzett's mother was on the lookout for a new formula for a cookie exchange and contest. "I said, 'Mom, I've got the perfect one,'" recalled Conzett, referring, of course, to Ricotta Sugar Cookies. "And she won with it."

MAKES 6 DOZEN COOKIES

FOR COOKIES

4 cups flour

2 tablespoons baking powder

1 teaspoon salt

1 cup (2 sticks) unsalted butter, at room
   temperature

2 cups granulated sugar

15 ounces ricotta cheese

2 teaspoons vanilla extract

2 eggs

FOR ICING

1 1/2 cups powdered sugar

3 tablespoons milk

Decorative sugar, optional

TO PREPARE COOKIES: Preheat the oven to 350°F and line the baking sheets with parchment paper.

In a medium bowl, whisk together the flour, baking powder, and salt, and reserve.

In the bowl of an electric mixer on medium-high speed, beat the butter until creamy, about 1 minute. Add the granulated sugar and beat until light and fluffy, about 2 minutes. Reduce the speed to medium, add the ricotta cheese, vanilla extract, and eggs, and beat until thoroughly combined. Reduce the speed to low, add the flour mixture, and mix until just combined and a dough forms.

Shape the dough into 1-inch balls, and place 2 inches apart on the prepared baking sheets. Bake until the cookies are lightly golden, about 15 minutes (the cookies will be soft). Remove the cookies from the oven and cool for 2 minutes before transferring them to a wire rack to cool completely.

TO PREPARE ICING: In a medium bowl, whisk together the powdered sugar and milk until smooth, adding more milk or powdered sugar as necessary for desired consistency. Using a small spatula or knife, spread the icing on the cookies (and garnish with the decorative sugar, optional). Allow the icing to set before serving.

Sambuca Chocolate Crinkles

Robert Bantle of St. Paul is a serious baker. "If I don't have at least ten pounds of flour in the house, I feel like something bad could happen," he said with a laugh. That explains why he buys the staple in twenty-five-pound quantities. And lots of chocolate: boxes with names such as Scharffen Berger, Valrhona, Guittard, and Ghirardelli line the pantry in his kitchen. Not that he eats it. "I never crave chocolate," Bantle said. "Or sweets. I'd rather eat a bag of Doritos. So it's hard to know why I like these cookies. Maybe it's that dark bittersweet chocolate, or maybe it's the surprise of the Sambuca's anise flavor." Or it could be the texture. "They have a really nice crunch on the outside," he said, which he believes is the result of allowing the cookies to cool completely on baking sheets. "But inside they're tender and moist, like a brownie."

MAKES 4 DOZEN COOKIES
12 ounces bittersweet chocolate
1 tablespoon unsalted butter
3 eggs
2 tablespoons Sambuca Black (see Note)
1 cup granulated sugar, divided
1 cup slivered almonds, finely chopped
2/3 cup flour
3/4 teaspoon baking soda
1/3 cup powdered sugar

NOTE This dough must be prepared in advance. Sambuca Black is an anise-flavored liqueur. This recipe works well when substituting gluten-free flour for all-purpose flour.

In a double boiler over gently simmering water (or in a bowl in a microwave oven), melt the chocolate and butter, whisking occasionally until smooth. Remove the chocolate mixture from the heat and cool slightly.

In a large bowl, whisk together the eggs, Sambuca Black, and 1/2 cup granulated sugar. Add the chocolate mixture and whisk until combined. Fold in the almonds, flour, and baking soda until combined; the dough will be soft and sticky. Cover the bowl with plastic wrap and refrigerate for at least 4 hours, or up to 24 hours.

When ready to bake, preheat the oven to 350°F and line the baking sheets with parchment paper.

In a shallow bowl, combine the remaining 1/2 cup granulated sugar and the powdered sugar. Shape the dough into 1-inch balls. Roll the cookies in the sugar mixture to coat and place 2 inches apart on the prepared baking sheets. Bake until the cookies are puffed, cracked, and just set, 10 to 12 minutes. Remove the cookies from the oven and cool completely on the baking sheets.

Snowball Clippers

Becky Varone of Chaska traces this recipe back to a coworker at an annual cookie exchange. For several years, a colleague supplied these coconut–chocolate cookies, and Varone asked for the recipe. "I was addicted to them," Varone said with a laugh. "I still have the original recipe in her handwriting. Now I make them every year at Christmas. My family loves them."

MAKES 4 TO 6 DOZEN COOKIES

1/2 cup flour
1/4 teaspoon baking powder
3/4 cup granulated sugar
1/3 cup sour cream
2 tablespoons unsalted butter, melted
1 egg white, lightly beaten
1/2 teaspoon vanilla extract
4 cups sweetened shredded coconut
1/2 cup miniature chocolate chips
4 ounces semisweet chocolate, melted

NOTE This recipe works well when substituting gluten-free flour for all-purpose flour.

Preheat the oven to 325°F and line the baking sheets with parchment paper.

In a small bowl, whisk together the flour and baking powder, and reserve.

In the bowl of an electric mixer on medium speed, beat the granulated sugar, sour cream, melted butter, and egg white until thoroughly combined. Reduce the speed to low, add the flour mixture, and mix until just combined. Add the vanilla extract and coconut, and mix until thoroughly combined. Stir in the chocolate chips.

Shape the dough into 1-inch balls and place 1 inch apart on the prepared baking sheets. Bake just until the coconut begins to brown, about 18 to 22 minutes. Remove the cookies from the oven and cool for 2 minutes before transferring them to a wire rack to cool completely.

Line the baking sheets with wax paper. Dip the bottoms of the cookies into the melted chocolate, and place the cookies, chocolate-side down, on wax paper. Refrigerate (about 30 minutes) to allow the chocolate to set before serving.

Strawberry Margarita Gems

"I'm a huge Food Network junkie," said Lance Swanson of North Branch. "I was watching Emeril make thumbprint cookies with raspberries and lemon zest, and I thought, 'That's wonderful, but what could I do that's different?' I like margaritas, so I thought, 'Strawberry and lime go together.' I putzed around until I found something I liked." Swanson doesn't use commercial jam in this recipe: he bakes from scratch. "I started helping my mom in the kitchen when I was a kid," he said. "I helped my mom measure flour, and I picked up tips and tricks. I like to challenge myself, give myself a goal. It's an excuse to experiment and it's a labor of love."

MAKES 3 TO 4 DOZEN COOKIES

FOR STRAWBERRY FILLING

1 pound frozen strawberries, thawed and chopped
1 cup granulated sugar
1 teaspoon freshly squeezed lime juice

FOR COOKIES

2 ¼ cups plus 2 tablespoons flour
1 teaspoon baking powder
¼ teaspoon salt
1 cup (2 sticks) unsalted butter, at room temperature
2/3 cup granulated sugar, plus extra for rolling dough
2 egg yolks
Freshly grated zest from 1 lime
2 teaspoons freshly squeezed lime juice
Flaky sea salt or coarse kosher salt, for decorating

NOTE This recipe must be prepared in advance. Strawberry jam can be substituted for the strawberry filling. Just add 1 teaspoon freshly grated lime zest to 1 cup prepared jam.

TO PREPARE STRAWBERRY FILLING: In a saucepan over medium heat, combine the strawberries and granulated sugar, and cook until the mixture is reduced to 1 cup. Remove the berry mixture from the heat, cool slightly, and stir in the lime juice. Transfer the mixture to a small bowl, cover with plastic wrap, and refrigerate overnight.

TO PREPARE COOKIES: Preheat the oven to 350°F and line the baking sheets with parchment paper.

In a medium bowl, whisk together the flour, baking powder, and salt, and reserve. In the bowl of an electric mixer on medium-high speed, beat the butter until creamy, about 1 minute. Add the granulated sugar and beat until light and fluffy, about 2 minutes. Add the egg yolks, one at a time, beating well after each addition. Add the lime zest and lime juice, and beat until thoroughly combined. Reduce the speed to low. Add the flour mixture in three additions, mixing until just combined.

Place some granulated sugar in a shallow bowl. Shape the dough into 1-inch balls. Roll the cookies in the granulated sugar to coat and place 2 inches apart on the prepared baking sheets. Using your finger or a ½-teaspoon measuring spoon, make a deep indentation in the center of each cookie, pressing together any cracks that may form. Fill the indentations with the strawberry filling (you will not use all the filling).

Bake until the cookies are golden brown on the bottom, 16 to 18 minutes. Remove the cookies from the oven and cool for 2 minutes before transferring them to a wire rack to cool completely. Top each cookie with a few grains of sea salt or kosher salt.

Sugar Plum Doodles

Using the standard snickerdoodle formula as a jumping-off point made perfect sense for friends Michelle Clark and Seamus Kirwin, both of Minneapolis. "It's Seamus's all-time favorite cookie," said Clark. "Plus, it's easy to make; it's accessible." The plum idea also came from Kirwin. "He had this vision to invoke the Sugar Plum Fairy from 'The Nutcracker,'" said Clark. "But he has zero baking background. I'm the one with the history and the love of baking. That's why we worked as a team on this."

MAKES 3 TO 4 DOZEN COOKIES

FOR PLUM FILLING

1 cup plum jam

⅛ teaspoon ground nutmeg

⅛ teaspoon ground cloves

⅛ teaspoon ground ginger

½ teaspoon ground cinnamon

FOR CINNAMON-SUGAR MIXTURE

¼ cup granulated sugar

1 tablespoon ground cinnamon

FOR COOKIES

1 teaspoon baking soda

1 teaspoon cream of tartar

½ teaspoon kosher salt

1 teaspoon ground cinnamon

2 ¾ cups flour

1 cup (2 sticks) unsalted butter, at room temperature

¾ cup granulated sugar

½ cup packed light brown sugar

1 egg

1 egg yolk

1 tablespoon vanilla extract

Decorative sugar

TO PREPARE PLUM FILLING: In a small saucepan over low heat, combine the plum jam, nutmeg, cloves, ginger and cinnamon, and cook until the mixture becomes thin (alternatively, combine in a microwave-safe bowl and heat in a microwave oven in a few 15-second bursts). Remove from the heat, and reserve.

TO PREPARE CINNAMON-SUGAR MIXTURE: In a shallow bowl, combine the granulated sugar and cinnamon, and reserve.

TO PREPARE COOKIES: Preheat the oven to 325°F and line the baking sheets with parchment paper.

In a medium bowl, whisk together the baking soda, cream of tartar, salt, 1 teaspoon cinnamon, and flour, and reserve.

In the bowl of an electric mixer on medium-high speed, beat the butter, granulated sugar, and brown sugar until light and fluffy, about 2 minutes. Add the egg, egg yolk, and vanilla extract and beat for 1 minute. Reduce the speed to low, add the flour mixture, and mix until just combined.

Shape the dough into 1-inch balls. Roll the cookies in the cinnamon-sugar mixture to coat and place 2 inches apart on the prepared baking sheets. Bake for 8 minutes. Remove from the oven. Using the back of a rounded spoon, make an indent in the center of each cookie. Fill the indent with 1 teaspoon of the plum filling and sprinkle with the decorative sugar. Return the baking sheet to the oven and bake until the cookies are lightly brown, an additional 3 to 4 minutes. Remove the cookies from the oven and cool for 5 minutes before transferring them to a wire rack to cool completely.

Swedish Almond Chocolate Macaroons

Beth Jones of Owatonna fell head-over-heels for this almond–chocolate treat when she was an exchange student in rural Sweden. Her host family always had this cookie on its shopping list, but Jones couldn't convince the store's baker to reveal the recipe. She set out to create it for herself, gleaning elements from three Swedish-language cookbooks and several Swedish baking websites. "I wanted mine to taste just like the ones I loved in Sweden," she said. "After a lot of practice, they finally do." Jones's research discovered another reason to appreciate this appealing cookie: it's flexible. "In Sweden, some are flavored with cognac or vanilla," she said. "This version is the one I had when I was there, so this is the version that I like. It's all to your own taste."

MAKES 2 TO 3 DOZEN COOKIES

FOR COOKIES

2 (7-ounce) tubes almond paste, cut into small pieces
2 egg whites
½ cup granulated sugar
Butter, for pressing dough

FOR FILLING

1 cup (2 sticks) unsalted butter, at room temperature
1 cup powdered sugar
2 teaspoons vanilla extract
2 tablespoons heavy cream
4 teaspoons unsweetened cocoa powder

FOR CHOCOLATE COATING

10 to 12 ounces dark or bittersweet chocolate
2 to 4 teaspoons vegetable oil or unsalted butter, melted

NOTE This dough must be prepared in advance. These Swedish cookies are also known as *Choklad Biskvier.*

TO PREPARE COOKIES: In the bowl of an electric mixer on medium speed, beat the almond paste and egg whites until thoroughly combined, about 2 minutes. Cover the bowl with plastic wrap and refrigerate for 30 minutes.

When ready to bake, preheat the oven to 350°F and line the baking sheets with parchment paper.

Shape the dough into 1-inch balls, and place 2 inches apart on the prepared baking sheets. Place the granulated sugar in a shallow bowl. Spread a light coating of butter on the flat bottom of a glass, dip it into the granulated sugar and carefully press the glass into a cookie, flattening it; repeat with the remaining cookies. Bake until lightly brown, 14 to 16 minutes. Remove the cookies from the oven and cool for 5 minutes before transferring them to a wire rack to cool completely.

TO PREPARE FILLING: Line the baking sheets with wax paper. In the bowl of an electric mixer on medium speed, beat the butter until creamy, about 1 minute. Add the powdered sugar, vanilla extract, heavy cream, and cocoa powder, and mix until smooth, about 2 minutes. Using a small knife, spread about 1 tablespoon of the filling on top of each cookie, making a rounded top. Transfer the cookies to the prepared baking sheets and refrigerate for at least 1 hour.

TO PREPARE CHOCOLATE COATING: Break the chocolate into small pieces. In a double boiler over gently simmering water (or in a bowl in a microwave oven), melt the chocolate, whisking occasionally until smooth. Whisk in 2 teaspoons of vegetable oil (or melted butter), adding more to reach the desired consistency. Remove from the heat and allow the mixture to cool for a few minutes; then dip the tops of the cookies into the chocolate mixture, holding onto the almond base. Return the cookies to the prepared baking sheets and refrigerate until the chocolate hardens, at least 30 minutes. Store in the refrigerator and serve chilled.

Swiss Chocolate Buttersweets

Surprisingly few people have asked Dianne Kemp of Chanhassen to share her recipe for Swiss Chocolate Buttersweets. Kemp theorizes that folks are put off by their baked-by-a-pro appearance. "They're not difficult to make, but they give the impression that they are," she said. This cheesecake-like cookie may not exactly shout "Deck the Halls," but a single taste reveals a highly appropriate level of celebratory overkill. "They're not the typical Christmas cookie, but they're decadent and creamy," she said. She makes them only in December. "I figure I should make people wait," she said, "and really want them."

MAKES 4 DOZEN COOKIES

FOR FILLING

8 ounces cream cheese, at room temperature

1 cup powdered sugar

1 1/2 teaspoons vanilla extract

1/4 cup flour

1/2 cup sweetened shredded coconut

1 cup chopped walnuts, optional

FOR COOKIES

2 1/4 cups flour

1/4 teaspoon salt

1 cup (2 sticks) unsalted butter, at room temperature

1 cup powdered sugar

2 teaspoons vanilla extract

FOR FROSTING

1 cup milk chocolate or semisweet chocolate chips

4 tablespoons (1/2 stick) unsalted butter

1 tablespoon light corn syrup

1 1/2 cups powdered sugar

1 cup chopped walnuts, optional

1/2 cup sweetened shredded coconut, optional

TO PREPARE FILLING: In the bowl of an electric mixer on medium-high speed, beat the cream cheese until creamy, about 1 minute. Gradually add the powdered sugar and beat until light and fluffy, about 2 minutes. Add the vanilla extract and beat until thoroughly combined. Reduce the speed to low, add the flour, and mix until just combined. Stir in the coconut. Stir in the walnuts (optional), and reserve.

TO PREPARE COOKIES: Preheat the oven to 350°F and line the baking sheets with parchment paper.

In a medium bowl, whisk together the flour and salt, and reserve. In the bowl of an electric mixer on medium-high speed, beat the butter until creamy, about 1 minute. Gradually add the powdered sugar and beat until light and fluffy, about 2 minutes. Add the vanilla extract and beat until thoroughly combined. Reduce the speed to low, add the flour mixture, and mix until just combined. Shape the dough into 1-inch balls, and place 2 inches apart on the prepared baking sheets. Using your thumb, make an indentation in the center of each cookie.

Bake until very lightly browned, 12 to 15 minutes. Remove the cookies from the oven and cool for 2 minutes before transferring them to a wire rack. While the cookies are still warm, fill the indentations with the cream cheese mixture. Cool cookies completely.

TO PREPARE FROSTING: In a double boiler over gently simmering water (or in a bowl in a microwave oven), combine the chocolate chips and butter, whisking occasionally

until smooth. Add the corn syrup and
2 tablespoons of water and whisk until
smooth. Add the powdered sugar and whisk
until smooth. Stir in the walnuts (optional),
and stir in the coconut (optional). Frost
each cookie. Allow the frosting to set before
serving.

Taffy Treats

Sherryl Joos of Plymouth described her first-place cookies to a T. "They grab the eye," she said. "People always say, 'Wow!' And they taste so good." She was right: The cookies grabbed the judges' eyes. And taste buds. Members of her family refer to the walnut–caramel treat as the "Toothpick Cookies," but Joos felt the familiar name had a low-wattage marquee value, so she improvised. But whatever Joos calls them, they're terrific and a staple of her holiday baking routine. In December, when she bakes ten dozen of her favorite cookies—inspired, at least in the looks department, by the candied apple—Joos will steer some into cookie exchanges and others into boxes for lucky recipients on her gift list. "A lot of friends get mad at me if I don't make them," she said. "They take a long time. But they're worth it."

MAKES 3 DOZEN COOKIES

FOR FILLING

1 ⅓ cups walnuts, divided

⅓ cup granulated sugar

⅓ cup evaporated milk

FOR COOKIES

½ cup (1 stick) unsalted butter, at room temperature

¼ cup packed light brown sugar

¼ cup powdered sugar

¼ teaspoon salt

1 egg

1 teaspoon vanilla extract

2 cups flour

Round, colored toothpicks

FOR CARAMEL COATING

1 (11-ounce) package caramels (such as the Kraft brand), unwrapped

½ cup evaporated milk

TO PREPARE FILLING: In a food processor fitted with a metal blade, pulse the walnuts until finely chopped. In a small saucepan over medium heat, combine ⅓ cup of the ground walnuts (reserve the remaining walnuts), granulated sugar, and evaporated milk, and cook, stirring constantly, until very thick, about 5 minutes. Remove the pan from the heat, cool, and reserve.

TO PREPARE COOKIES: Preheat the oven to 350°F and line the baking sheets with parchment paper.

In the bowl of an electric mixer on medium-high speed, beat the butter until creamy, about 1 minute. Add the brown sugar, powdered sugar, and salt, and beat until light and fluffy, about 2 minutes. Add the egg and vanilla extract, and beat until thoroughly combined. Reduce the speed to low, add the flour, and mix until just combined.

Shape the dough into 1-inch balls. Make a depression in each cookie with your thumb and spoon ¼ teaspoon filling into the depression. Reshape the cookie into a ball, enclosing the filling. Place the cookies 2 inches apart on the prepared baking sheets and bake until lightly browned, 15 to 18 minutes. Remove the cookies from the oven and cool for 2 minutes before transferring them to a wire rack. Insert a rounded, colored wooden toothpick into the top of each cookie and cool completely.

TO PREPARE CARAMEL COATING: In a double boiler over gently simmering water (or in a bowl in a microwave oven), combine the caramels and evaporated milk. Heat until the caramels melt, stirring occasionally; if too thick, thin the mixture with water,

1 teaspoon at a time, until the caramel coating reaches spreading consistency. Remove from the heat but keep the caramel coating warm over hot water. Dip each cookie into the caramel coating, allowing the excess to drop off (the cookies can be double-dipped), and then dip the bottom of the caramel-coated cookie into the remaining 1 cup ground walnuts. Place the cookies on wax paper or parchment paper and allow the caramel coating to set before serving.

Whiskey Gingers

A beloved church cookbook was the creative starting point for Janet Heirigs of Minneapolis. "It's from the church where my dad grew up," she said. "There are at least our ginger cookies in that cookbook, and I chose the recipe from my dad's cousin. Then I started taking things out and putting things in." The "putting-things-in" part included whiskey. "I love ginger, and I love ginger ale," said Heirigs. "When my mom and I traveled to Ireland, we squeezed in a stop at a distillery, and had a whiskey and ginger. It's a good drink, and it got me thinking that it might be a good cookie."

MAKES 3 DOZEN COOKIES

FOR COOKIES

2 1/2 cups flour
2 teaspoons ground ginger
2 teaspoons baking soda
1/4 teaspoon salt
3/4 cup (1 1/2 sticks) unsalted butter, at room
    temperature
1 cup packed dark brown sugar
1 egg
2 tablespoons whiskey (see Note)
1 tablespoon freshly grated ginger root
2/3 cup finely chopped crystallized ginger
    (about 3 ounces), divided

FOR GINGER-SUGAR MIXTURE

1 teaspoon ground ginger
1/2 cup granulated sugar

FOR WHISKEY-GLAZED CASHEWS

1 teaspoon maple syrup
1/2 teaspoon whiskey
1 teaspoon ginger-sugar mixture
Pinch of kosher salt
3/4 cup whole cashews, unsalted or salted

FOR ICING

1 tablespoon unsalted butter, at room
    temperature
2 tablespoons cream cheese, at room
    temperature
1 teaspoon ground ginger
1 1/2 teaspoons whiskey
2 cups powdered sugar
1 to 6 teaspoons half-and-half or milk,
    divided

NOTE This dough must be prepared in advance. Bourbon can be substituted for whiskey.

TO PREPARE COOKIES: In a medium bowl, whisk together the flour, ground ginger, baking soda, and salt, and reserve.

In the bowl of an electric mixer on medium-high speed, beat butter until creamy, about 1 minute. Add the brown sugar and beat until light and fluffy, about 2 minutes. Add the egg, whiskey, and grated ginger root and mix until thoroughly combined. Reduce the speed to low, add the flour mixture, and mix until just combined. Stir in the crystallized ginger. Cover the bowl with plastic wrap and refrigerate for at least 2 hours, or overnight.

TO PREPARE GINGER-SUGAR MIXTURE: In a small bowl, combine the ground ginger and granulated sugar, reserving 1 teaspoon for glazing cashews.

TO PREPARE WHISKEY-GLAZED CASHEWS: Preheat the oven to 325°F and line a rimmed baking sheet with parchment paper. In a medium bowl, combine the maple syrup, whiskey, reserved 1 teaspoon ginger-sugar mixture, and kosher salt. Toss the cashews in the whiskey mixture until well-coated. Spread the cashews on the prepared baking sheet and bake until golden, about 6 to 8 minutes. Remove the cashews from the oven and cool completely. Chop the cashews into small pieces, and reserve.

TO ASSEMBLE COOKIES: When ready to bake, preheat the oven to 350°F and line the baking sheets with parchment paper. Place a wire rack over wax paper or parchment paper.

Shape the dough into 1-inch balls. Dip the top half of each cookie into ginger-sugar mixture and place 2 inches apart on the prepared baking sheets. Bake until the edges are lightly brown and the tops are slightly cracked, about 8 to 10 minutes. Remove the cookies from the oven and cool for 2 minutes before transferring them to a wire rack to cool completely.

TO PREPARE ICING: In the bowl of an electric mixer on medium-high speed, beat the butter, cream cheese, ground ginger, and whiskey until creamy. Reduce the speed to low and slowly add the powdered sugar. Add the half-and-half (or milk), 1 teaspoon at a time (and up to 6 teaspoons), to reach the desired consistency.

TO FINISH COOKIES: In a small bowl, stir together the remaining ⅓ cup crystallized ginger with the chopped whiskey-glazed cashews. Spread the icing on the top of each cookie, then sprinkle the ginger-cashews mixture over the icing. Allow the icing to set before serving.

White Chocolate–Cherry Tea Cakes

Teri Laster of Bloomington doctored a friend's familiar Russian tea cakes recipe with ingredients she happened to have on hand: white chocolate and dried cherries. "The cherries are a good fit, because the tartness is such a nice surprise," she said. "Everyone seemed to enjoy them, and so I've been making them that way ever since." Laster's innovations also involve skipping the cookie's traditional double-dip of powdered sugar. "It's such a heavy coating," she said. "That's why I started just sprinkling a little powdered sugar on top."

MAKES 3 DOZEN COOKIES

1 cup (2 sticks) unsalted butter, at room temperature

1/2 cup powdered sugar, plus extra for garnish

1 teaspoon vanilla extract

2 1/4 cups flour

1/2 teaspoon kosher salt

1/2 cup finely chopped pecans

1/2 cup chopped dried cherries

4 ounces white chocolate, chopped

Preheat the oven to 375°F and line the baking sheets with parchment paper. Place a wire rack over wax paper or parchment paper.

In the bowl of an electric mixer on medium-high speed, beat the butter and powdered sugar until light and fluffy, about 2 minutes. Add the vanilla extract and beat until thoroughly combined. Reduce the speed to low, add the flour and salt, and mix until just combined (the dough will seem crumbly). Stir in the pecans, cherries, and white chocolate.

Shape the dough into 1-inch balls, and place 2 inches apart on the prepared baking sheets, pressing the top of the dough slightly. Bake until the cookies just set and start to brown, about 9 to 11 minutes. Remove the cookies from the oven and cool for 5 minutes before transferring them to the prepared wire rack to cool completely. Dust with powdered sugar.

CONTENTS

CHAPTER THREE

THE ULTIMATE MINNESOTA COOKIE BOOK

Cutout Cookies

Chai Crescents

Every year, Lisa Osacho's Eden Prairie kitchen becomes Christmas Cookie Baking Central, when her family gathers and bakes for the holidays. One favorite is a buttery, delicate-as-pie-crust delight from her mother's yuletide baking routine. Even a beloved family classic isn't off limits to Osacho's tinkering, this time involving a chai formula from a magazine of Lunds & Byerlys supermarkets. "I like to put a modern twist on recipes, make my own concoctions," she said. "These remind me of a really, really good version of pecan sandies," said one of our judges. "I always loved those cookies."

MAKES 2 DOZEN COOKIES

FOR COOKIES

1/2 cup (1 stick) unsalted butter, at room temperature

3 tablespoons granulated sugar

1 teaspoon vanilla extract

1 cup flour, plus extra for rolling dough

Pinch of salt

1/2 cup finely chopped pecans or walnuts, toasted (see Note)

FOR CHAI SPICE BLEND

1/4 teaspoon ground cloves

1/2 teaspoon ground cardamom

1/2 teaspoon ground ginger

1/4 teaspoon ground white pepper

1/2 teaspoon ground cinnamon

2/3 cup superfine sugar

NOTE This dough must be prepared in advance. To toast pecans or walnuts, place the nuts in a dry skillet over medium heat and cook, stirring (or shaking the pan frequently), until they just begin to release their fragrance, about 3 to 4 minutes (alternately, preheat oven to 325°F, spread the nuts on an ungreased baking sheet, and bake, stirring often, for 4 to 6 minutes). Remove the nuts from the heat and cool to room temperature.

TO PREPARE COOKIES: In the bowl of an electric mixer on medium-high speed, beat the butter until creamy, about 1 minute. Add the granulated sugar and beat until light and fluffy, about 1 minute. Add the vanilla extract and beat until thoroughly combined. Reduce the speed to low, add the flour and salt, and mix until just combined. Stir in the chopped nuts. Form the dough into a disk, wrap in plastic wrap, and refrigerate at least 4 hours, or overnight.

TO PREPARE CHAI SPICE BLEND: In a small bowl, whisk together the cloves, cardamom, ginger, white pepper, cinnamon, and superfine sugar, and reserve.

TO ASSEMBLE COOKIES: When ready to bake, preheat the oven to 350°F and line the baking sheets with parchment paper. Place a wire rack over wax paper or parchment paper.

On a lightly floured surface using a lightly floured rolling pin, roll the dough to 1/4-inch thickness. Using a crescent-shaped cookie cutter, cut the dough into crescents, and place 1 inch apart on the prepared baking sheets. Repeat with the remaining dough, gathering up the scraps, re-rolling, and cutting until all the dough is used. Bake until golden brown on the bottom, about 10 minutes. Remove the cookies from the oven and cool for 2 minutes before transferring them to a wire rack to cool for an additional 5 minutes. While they are still warm, carefully dip the cookies in the chai spice blend and transfer them to the prepared wire rack to cool completely.

Cherry Almond Turnovers

"I love experimenting in the kitchen," said Lance Swanson of North Branch. "It's the mad scientist in me. I'm happiest in the kitchen. Baking is my meditative time." This recipe came about after he saw cherry turnovers in a bakery: "I thought that would make a good idea for a cookie."

MAKES 4 DOZEN COOKIES

FOR FILLING

1/2 cup granulated sugar

2 tablespoons cornstarch

1/2 cup sour cherry juice

3/4 cup minced dried tart cherries

1/2 cup finely grated almond paste

FOR COOKIES

2 cups chilled flour, plus extra for rolling dough

2 rounded tablespoons granulated sugar

1/4 teaspoon salt

3/4 cup (1 1/2 sticks) cold unsalted butter, diced

2 ounces cold cream cheese, cut into 1/2-inch pieces

1 egg, beaten

Decorative sugar or granulated sugar

NOTE This dough must be prepared in advance.

TO PREPARE FILLING: In a small saucepan over high heat, whisk together the granulated sugar and cornstarch. Whisk in the cherry juice and bring the mixture to a boil. Cook until thick, about 1 minute. Remove the pan from the heat, transfer the filling to a heatproof bowl, and cool to room temperature. Fold in the cherries and almond paste. Cover the bowl with plastic wrap and refrigerate for at least 1 hour.

TO PREPARE COOKIES: In a food processor fitted with a metal blade, combine the flour, granulated sugar, and salt, and pulse until combined. Add the butter and cream cheese, and pulse until the mixture resembles coarse crumbs. Add 6 to 7 tablespoons of ice water, 1 tablespoon at a time, and pulse until the dough starts to form marble-size clumps. Divide the dough into 2 equal pieces. Form the dough into disks, wrap in plastic wrap, and refrigerate for 1 hour.

When ready to bake, preheat the oven to 400°F and line the baking sheets with parchment paper. Work with half the dough at a time, remove the dough from the refrigerator and allow to stand for 5 minutes.

On a lightly floured surface using a lightly floured rolling pin, roll the dough to 1/16-inch thickness (the dough will be quite elastic). Using a knife or a cookie cutter, cut out 2 1/2-inch squares or circles and place them 1 inch apart on the prepared baking sheets. Repeat with the remaining dough, gathering up scraps, re-rolling, and cutting until all the dough is used.

Drop 1 teaspoon filling in the center of each square. Brush the edges of the cookies with the beaten egg, carefully fold the dough over the filling to form a triangle, and press the edges to seal (the cookies may be refrigerated at this point until ready to bake). Brush the tops of the cookies with the beaten egg and sprinkle with decorative or granulated sugar.

Bake until light golden brown, 17 to 19 minutes. Remove the cookies from the oven and cool for 2 minutes before transferring them to a wire rack to cool completely.

Cherry Pinwheels

Baking has been a lifelong avocation for Pam Hopf of Edina. "I started baking when I could barely reach the counter," she said. "My mother was a very good baker, and by the time I was eight years old, I was helping. When I got older, every time she'd leave the house, I'd bake something. I didn't like the supervision. Whatever I made usually turned out well, so that was my encouragement to keep going." The recipe, which Hopf encountered in *Gourmet* magazine, sounds complicated, but it is not as hard as it looks.

MAKES 2 DOZEN COOKIES

2 1/2 cups flour, plus extra for rolling dough
1/2 teaspoon salt
3/4 teaspoon ground cardamom
1 cup (2 sticks) unsalted butter, at room temperature
4 ounces cream cheese, at room temperature
1 cup granulated sugar
1 egg, separated
1 teaspoon vanilla extract
1/3 cup cherry preserves
2 tablespoons decorative sugar

NOTE This dough must be prepared in advance. Not a fan of cherry? Almost any fruit preserve works with this festive cookie.

In a medium bowl, whisk together the flour, salt, and cardamom, and reserve. In the bowl of an electric mixer on medium-high speed, beat the butter and cream cheese until creamy, about 1 minute. Add the granulated sugar and beat until light and fluffy, about 2 minutes. Add the egg yolk and vanilla extract, and beat until thoroughly combined. Reduce the speed to low. Add the flour mixture in three additions, mixing until just combined and a dough forms. Divide the dough into four equal pieces. Form the dough into rectangles, wrap in plastic wrap, and refrigerate for 3 hours.

When ready to bake, preheat the oven to 350°F and line the baking sheets with parchment paper.

On a lightly floured surface using a lightly floured rolling pin, roll the dough blocks (one at a time, keeping the remaining dough refrigerated until ready to roll) to 1/4-inch thickness. Working quickly (the dough is easiest to work with when chilled), trim the edges to make an 8- by 12-inch rectangle. Rewrap the scraps in plastic and refrigerate until ready to re-roll.

Using a pastry wheel, cut the rectangle into 2-inch squares. Using a spatula, transfer the squares to the prepared baking sheets, placing them 2 inches apart. With a small knife, carefully make a 1-inch-long cut in one square, from the tip of each corner in toward the center, halving each corner (you will have eight points). With the tip of the knife, lift every other point and gently fold into the center (forming a pinwheel), overlapping the ends slightly. Press the center lightly to form a small well. In a small bowl, lightly whisk the reserved egg white with a fork. Brush the cookies with the egg white. Place 1/2 teaspoon of cherry preserves in the center and sprinkle with decorative sugar. Repeat this process with the remaining chilled dough and scraps.

Bake until the edges are pale and golden, 10 to 15 minutes. Remove the cookies from the oven and cool for 5 minutes before transferring them to a wire rack to cool completely.

Cranberry Cornmeal Shortbread Cookies

"To me, this cookie just looks like the holidays," said Mary Martin of Minneapolis. "It's the cranberries, and the rosemary, and the orange glaze. Baking is a gift to your company. You put a little love into it." Martin's affection for cornmeal—the cookie's secret weapon—is based on the happy memories of her Virginia grandmother's kitchen. "My baking roots come from her," she said. "Cornmeal is the South, and Southerners like cornbread. For as long as I can remember, my grandmother would make cornbread. She'd crumple it up and add milk and sugar, and it was wonderful."

MAKES 2½ DOZEN 2-INCH RECTANGLE COOKIES

FOR GLAZE

⅓ cup powdered sugar

1 teaspoon freshly grated orange zest

2 to 4 teaspoons freshly squeezed orange juice

FOR COOKIES

1 cup flour, plus extra for rolling dough

¼ cup finely ground yellow cornmeal

3 tablespoons granulated sugar

1 to 2 teaspoons freshly chopped rosemary

Pinch of cayenne pepper

½ cup (1 stick) unsalted butter, chilled and cut into small pieces

2 to 4 tablespoons chopped dried cranberries

NOTE This dough must be prepared in advance. Use more or less rosemary and dried cranberries, according to your preferences. If you prefer not to bother with cookie cutters, simply form the dough into a ball (do not refrigerate), shape it into a flat 8-inch circle on the prepared baking sheet, and score into 16 wedges. Poke each wedge at least twice with a fork. Bake as directed; then rescore the cookies, cool, and glaze.

TO PREPARE GLAZE: In a medium bowl, whisk together the powdered sugar, orange zest, and 2 teaspoons orange juice, adding more orange juice, a teaspoon at a time, until the glaze is slightly runny. Reserve.

TO PREPARE COOKIES: In a large bowl, whisk together the flour, cornmeal, granulated sugar, rosemary, and cayenne. Using a pastry blender or fork, cut in the butter until the mixture resembles coarse meal. (You may need to add water, ½ teaspoon at a time, to help the dough come together.) Stir in the dried cranberries. Form the dough into a disk, wrap in plastic wrap, and refrigerate for at least 1 hour.

When ready to bake, preheat the oven to 325°F and line the baking sheets with parchment paper.

On a lightly floured surface using a lightly floured rolling pin, roll the dough to ¼-inch thickness. Use cookie cutters to cut the dough and place the cookies 2 inches apart on the prepared baking sheets. Repeat with the remaining dough, gathering up scraps, re-rolling, and cutting until all the dough is used.

Bake until lightly brown, 21 to 24 minutes. Remove the cookies from the oven and cool on the baking sheets for 5 minutes. Brush the cookies with the glaze; then transfer the cookies to a wire rack to cool completely.

Cranberry-Filled Cookies

Wendy Nickel of Kiester got the idea for this recipe after a visit to a Wisconsin cranberry festival, where she was inspired by all the tempting uses she encountered for the bright red autumn berry. She went back home determined to find more ways to incorporate cranberries into her cooking. That's when she remembered the beloved raisin-filled cookie baked by her husband's grandmother. "If raisins work, why not cranberries?" she said. "I like to see what works and what doesn't. During the holidays, I love the smell of cranberries and oranges."

MAKES 4 DOZEN COOKIES

2 ½ cups flour, plus extra for rolling dough

1 teaspoon baking powder

¼ teaspoon salt

1 cup (2 sticks) unsalted butter, at room temperature

1 ½ cups granulated sugar, divided

2 teaspoons vanilla extract

1 egg

1 ½ cups dried cranberries

1 tablespoon freshly grated orange zest

2 tablespoons cornstarch

NOTE This dough must be prepared in advance.

In a medium bowl, whisk together the flour, baking powder, and salt, and reserve. In the bowl of an electric mixer on medium-high speed, beat the butter until creamy, about 1 minute. Add 1 cup granulated sugar and beat until light and fluffy, about 2 minutes. Add the vanilla extract and beat until thoroughly combined. Add the egg and beat until thoroughly combined. Reduce the speed to low, add the flour mixture, and mix until just combined. Cover the bowl with plastic wrap and refrigerate for at least 2 hours.

In a small saucepan over medium-high heat, combine the remaining ½ cup granulated sugar, cranberries, orange zest, 1 ½ cups water, and cornstarch, and cook, stirring occasionally, until thickened, about 5 minutes. Remove from the heat and cool.

When ready to bake, preheat the oven to 375°F and line the baking sheets with parchment paper.

On a lightly floured surface using a lightly floured rolling pin, roll the dough to ⅛-inch thickness. Cut the dough into 3-inch circles, placing them 2 inches apart on the prepared baking sheets. Repeat with the remaining dough, gathering up the scraps, re-rolling, and cutting them until all the dough is used.

Place 1 heaping teaspoon of the cranberry mixture into the center of each cookie. Fold the edges of the dough toward the center, leaving most of the cranberry mixture uncovered. Bake until lightly browned, 12 to 15 minutes. Remove the cookies from the oven and cool for 2 minutes before transferring them to a wire rack to cool completely.

Ginger Creams

One of Patricia Bauer's happiest childhood memories is the big clear glass cookie jar in the kitchen of her grandmother's Wisconsin farm, which Eva Greismer kept stocked with giant molasses cookies glazed with sweet icing. "I remember making Ginger Creams every year for Christmas, using all of the holiday cookie cutters that we had accumulated over the years," she said. Today, Bauer, who lives in Minneapolis, follows a less-is-more approach. "Even though I have probably forty or fifty cookie cutters, the main one I use is the top ring from a canning jar."

MAKES 3 DOZEN COOKIES

FOR COOKIES

1 cup (2 sticks) unsalted butter, at room temperature

1 cup granulated sugar

2 eggs

1 cup molasses

2 teaspoons ground cinnamon

2 teaspoons ground ginger

1 teaspoon baking soda

1 teaspoon cream of tartar

3 ½ to 4 cups flour, plus extra for rolling dough

1 cup sour cream

FOR ICING

4 tablespoons (½ stick) unsalted butter, at room temperature

1 teaspoon vanilla extract

½ cup milk

4 cups powdered sugar

Food coloring and decorative sugar, optional

NOTE This dough must be prepared in advance. When choosing cookie cutters for this recipe, keep the shapes simple. The dough will stick to intricate cutters.

TO PREPARE COOKIES: In the bowl of an electric mixer on medium-high speed, beat the butter until creamy, about 1 minute. Add the granulated sugar and beat until light and fluffy, about 2 minutes. Add the eggs, one at a time, beating well after each addition. Add the molasses, cinnamon, ginger, baking soda, and cream of tartar, and beat until thoroughly combined. Reduce the speed to low. Add the flour in three additions, alternating with the sour cream, beginning with the flour and ending with the sour cream. Mix until just combined (if the dough is really sticky, add extra flour, 1 tablespoon at a time). Cover the bowl with plastic wrap and refrigerate overnight.

When ready to bake, preheat the oven to 350°F and line the baking sheets with parchment paper.

Lightly flour a surface and your hands. Take a handful of the dough and press it down on the prepared surface; then flip the dough and press again, so there is flour on both flat sides of the dough. Using a lightly floured rolling pin, roll the dough to ¼-inch thickness. Dip the cookie cutters in the flour, cut the dough into desired shapes, and place 2 inches apart on the prepared baking sheets (grouping similar-size cookies on the same baking sheet to avoid burning). Repeat with the remaining dough, gathering up the scraps, re-rolling, and cutting until all the dough is used.

Bake until the cookies have puffed up a bit and a lightly pressed finger doesn't leave an indentation, about 10 minutes. Remove the cookies from the oven and cool for 2 minutes before transferring them to a wire rack to cool completely.

TO PREPARE ICING: In the bowl of an electric mixer on medium-high speed, beat the butter and vanilla extract until fluffy. Add the milk and beat until thoroughly combined. Reduce the speed to low and add the powdered sugar, 1 cup at a time, until the icing reaches a desired consistency. Add the food coloring (optional), one drop at a time, and mix until thoroughly combined. Using a knife, spread the icing on the cookies (this recipe makes a generous amount of icing) and sprinkle with the decorative sugar (optional).

Kolaches

Pat Monson Johnson of Eden Prairie said that these beauties were a beloved standard in her mother's kitchen. "I'll be making these kolaches until I can't make cookies any longer," she said. "They're more like a mini-pastry, a glorified cookie. I'll go to a nice bakery and see kolaches and I'll think, 'Oh, no, they won't be as good as my cookie.'" Probably not.

MAKES 5 DOZEN COOKIES

4 cups flour, plus extra for rolling dough
1 envelope (¼ ounce) active dry yeast
2 cups (4 sticks) cold unsalted butter,
   cut into small pieces
2 egg yolks
1 cup sour cream
3 egg whites
1 cup granulated sugar
About 2 cups apricot or raspberry preserves
Powdered sugar, for garnish

NOTE This dough must be prepared in advance. This cookie recipe is based on the Eastern European sweet yeast buns of the same name (pronounced koh-LAH-cheez). These cookies freeze beautifully.

In a large bowl, sift the flour. Sprinkle the yeast over the flour. Using a pastry cutter or fork, cut the butter into the flour until the mixture resembles coarse meal. Add the egg yolks and sour cream, and stir until well-combined (the dough will be thick). Cover the bowl with plastic wrap and refrigerate for at least 4 hours, or overnight.

When ready to bake, preheat the oven to 350°F and line the baking sheets with parchment paper.

Place a wire rack over wax paper or parchment paper. In the bowl of an electric mixer fitted with a whisk attachment on medium-high speed, whip the egg whites until they form soft peaks. Slowly add the granulated sugar and continue to whip until the meringue forms stiff, glossy (but not dry) peaks, and reserve.

On a lightly floured surface using a lightly floured rolling pin, roll 1 cup of cookie dough (keeping the remaining dough in the refrigerator so it remains firm) to the thickness of a pie crust, roughly ⅛- to ¼-inch thick. Using a 3-inch cookie cutter or a pastry or pizza cutter, cut the dough into 3-inch squares and place them 2 inches apart on the prepared baking sheets. Repeat with the remaining dough, gathering up the scraps, re-rolling, and cutting until all the dough is used.

Fill each square with ¾ teaspoon of fruit preserves and 1 generous teaspoon of meringue. Pull the corners of the cookie into the center and pinch the gathered corners together tightly. Bake the cookies until the pastry is golden brown (the cookies will reopen during baking), about 25 minutes. Remove the cookies from the oven and cool for 2 minutes before transferring them to the prepared wire rack to cool completely. Dust with powdered sugar.

Lemon–Lime Christmas Trees

Baking is a labor of love for Joan Hause of Lake Elmo. "I love making cookies," she said. "I'm known in our family as 'the baker.'" She bakes a lot of Christmas cookies: "I'm big on the standards, but I play with recipes to make my own version. I adapted this recipe from lemon sugar cookies. I like the flavor of lime." With Hause, appearances matter: "I was happy that these cookies taste as good as they look."

MAKES 4 DOZEN COOKIES

FOR COOKIES

3 ¾ cups flour, plus extra for rolling dough
1 teaspoon baking powder
1 teaspoon baking soda
¼ teaspoon salt
1 cup (2 sticks) unsalted butter, at room temperature
1 ½ cups granulated sugar
2 eggs
2 tablespoons freshly squeezed lemon juice
2 teaspoons lemon extract
1 teaspoon yellow food coloring, optional

FOR ICING

3 ounces cream cheese, at room temperature
3 tablespoons unsalted butter, at room temperature
2 cups powdered sugar
½ teaspoon freshly grated lime zest
1 tablespoon freshly squeezed lime juice
1 teaspoon green food coloring
Decorative sugar, optional

NOTE This dough must be prepared in advance. The dough tends to be sticky, so when rolling it out, work quickly, keeping a liberal amount of flour on both the work surface and on the rolling pin.

TO PREPARE COOKIES: In a medium bowl, whisk together the flour, baking powder, baking soda, and salt, and reserve. In the bowl of an electric mixer on medium speed, beat the butter until creamy, about 1 minute. Add the granulated sugar and beat until light and fluffy, about 2 minutes. Add the

eggs, one at a time, beating well after each addition. Add the lemon juice, lemon extract, and yellow food coloring (optional), and beat until thoroughly combined. Reduce the speed to low, add the flour mixture, and mix until just combined. Divide the dough into 2 equal pieces. Form the dough into disks, wrap in plastic wrap, and refrigerate for at least 2 hours.

When ready to bake, preheat the oven to 350°F and line the baking sheets with parchment paper.

On a lightly floured surface using a lightly floured rolling pin, roll the dough to ¼-inch thickness. Using a tree cookie cutter, cut the dough and place 2 inches apart on the prepared baking sheets. Repeat with the remaining dough, gathering up scraps, re-rolling, and cutting until all the dough is used. Bake until the cookies are set but not hard, 9 to 10 minutes. Remove the cookies from the oven and cool for 2 minutes before transferring them to a wire rack to cool completely.

TO PREPARE ICING: In the bowl of an electric mixer on medium speed, beat the cream cheese and butter until creamy, about 1 minute. Reduce the speed to low, add the powdered sugar, and mix until creamy, about 2 minutes. Add the lime zest, lime juice, and food coloring, and mix until thoroughly combined. Ice the cookies, and garnish with the decorative sugar (optional).

Minnesota Sundae Cookies

When Kristi Hanson of Minneapolis was growing up in northern Minnesota, she looked forward to the annual Beltrami County Fair. "There was a stand serving sundaes, big scoops of vanilla ice cream topped with honey and sunflower seeds." Hanson recalled that they were dubbed "Minnesota Sundaes," because the stand was promoting Minnesota-made products. "We thought it was the greatest thing, and I thought that the combination would make a great cookie," she said. "I like the creativity of making my own recipes."

MAKES 3 TO 4 DOZEN COOKIES

FOR COOKIES

3 cups flour, plus extra for rolling dough

1 teaspoon baking powder

1/2 teaspoon salt

1 cup (2 sticks) butter, at room temperature

1 cup granulated sugar

1 egg

2 tablespoons half-and-half or milk

1 teaspoon vanilla extract

1 teaspoon vanilla bean paste (see Note)

FOR HONEY BUTTERCREAM ICING

1/4 cup honey

2 tablespoons butter, at room temperature

3 cups powdered sugar

1 to 4 tablespoons half-and-half or milk

1/2 cup toasted and salted sunflower seeds

Decorative sprinkles, optional

NOTE This dough must be prepared in advance. As a substitute for vanilla bean paste, cut a vanilla bean lengthwise, split it open, scrape the seeds into the dough, and discard the vanilla bean.

TO PREPARE COOKIES: In a medium bowl, whisk together the flour, baking powder, and salt, and reserve.

In the bowl of an electric mixer on medium-high speed, beat the butter and granulated sugar until light and fluffy, about 2 minutes. Add the egg, half-and-half (or milk), vanilla extract, and vanilla bean paste (or vanilla bean seeds), and mix until thoroughly combined. Reduce the speed to low, add the flour mixture, and mix until just combined. Form the dough into a disk, wrap in plastic wrap, and refrigerate for at least 1 hour.

When ready to bake, preheat the oven to 350°F and line the baking sheets with parchment paper.

On a lightly floured surface using a lightly floured rolling pin, roll the dough to 1/4-inch thickness. Use a cutter to cut shapes and place 2 inches apart on the prepared baking sheets. Repeat with the remaining dough, gathering up the scraps, re-rolling and cutting until all the dough is used. Bake until the edges are lightly browned, about 8 to 10 minutes. Remove the cookies from the oven and cool for 2 minutes before transferring them to a wire rack to cool completely.

TO PREPARE HONEY BUTTERCREAM ICING:
In a medium bowl, stir the honey and butter into the powdered sugar until it gets too stiff to stir. Add the half-and-half (or milk), 1 tablespoon at a time and up to 4 tablespoons, until the desired spreading consistency develops. Spread the icing across the top of each cookie, then garnish the tops with the sunflower seeds and the decorative sprinkles (optional). The icing sets up rather quickly, so it's best to add the toppings to each cookie as it is iced.

Orange Chocolate Cookies

The heaven-made marriage of chocolate and orange has always caught the attention of Eileen Troxel of St. Paul. "I have loved that combination ever since I was little," she said. "It started with orange sherbet and chocolate sauce." That explains why, while thumbing through *Traditional Home* magazine a few years ago, she was immediately drawn to a butter cookie flavored with orange zest, decorated with orange marmalade, and dipped in bittersweet chocolate. The recipe quickly ascended to the top of Troxel's December baking routine. Troxel is a year-round baker, although cookies make a strictly seasonal appearance. "I leave cookies to Christmas," she said. "That makes them special."

MAKES 3 DOZEN COOKIES

1 cup (2 sticks) unsalted butter, at room
　temperature, plus extra for chocolate
　dipping sauce
1 cup granulated sugar
1 egg yolk
2 teaspoons freshly grated orange zest
2 cups flour, plus extra for rolling dough
1/4 cup orange marmalade, divided
6 ounces bittersweet chocolate

Preheat the oven to 375°F and line the baking sheets with parchment paper.

In the bowl of an electric mixer on medium-high speed, beat the butter until creamy, about 1 minute. Add the granulated sugar and beat until light and fluffy, about 2 minutes. Add the egg yolk and orange zest, and beat until thoroughly combined. Reduce the speed to low, add the flour, and mix until just combined.

On a lightly floured surface using a lightly floured rolling pin, roll the dough to 1/4-inch thickness. Using a 1 1/2-inch round cookie cutter, cut the dough into rounds, and place 1 inch apart on the prepared baking sheets. Repeat with the remaining dough, gathering up the scraps, re-rolling, and cutting until all the dough is used. Using your thumb, make a slight indentation in the center of the cookie and fill with 1/4 teaspoon orange marmalade. Bake until the edges are lightly browned, about 12 minutes. Remove the cookies from the oven and cool for 2 minutes before transferring them to a wire rack to cool completely.

In a double boiler over gently simmering water (or in a bowl in a microwave oven), melt the chocolate, whisking in enough butter (1 tablespoon at a time, up to about 4 tablespoons) to make a good dipping consistency. Dip half of each cookie in the chocolate and place on wax paper until the chocolate sets.

Smoky Blue-Cheese Cherry Cookies

While working on a food science and technology master's degree at the University of Wisconsin–Stout, Kylie White of Shorewood studied the use of black teas as flavoring agents in shortbread cookies. "Then I started tinkering," she said. "This recipe started off as a basic shortbread cookie with black tea ground up in it. But then I went to a class on cooking and baking with tea, and that's where I learned about steeping tea in butter. It incorporates the tea flavor so much better. You don't end up with bits of tea leaves in the dough."

MAKES 2 TO 3 DOZEN COOKIES

1/2 cup (1 stick) butter, melted

1 tablespoon loose-leaf Lapsang Souchong tea (see Note)

1 1/2 cups flour, plus extra for rolling dough

1 1/2 teaspoons kosher salt

1 teaspoon freshly ground black pepper

2 ounces blue cheese, crumbled

2 ounces dried cherries, chopped

1 egg

1/4 cup heavy cream, plus extra if needed

NOTE This dough must be prepared in advance. Lapsang Souchong is a smoky-flavored tea.

In a small bowl, combine the melted butter and tea leaves and allow to steep for 5 to 10 minutes, depending on taste. Pour the melted butter through a fine mesh strainer into a small bowl, discarding the tea leaves. Cover the butter with plastic wrap and refrigerate for at least 1 hour.

In a large bowl, whisk together the flour, salt, and pepper. Cut the tea butter into small pieces. Using a pastry cutter or fork, cut the tea butter into the flour mixture, until the dough is crumbly. Fold in the blue cheese and cherries.

In a small bowl, whisk together the egg and cream. Stir the egg mixture into the flour mixture until just combined. You may need to add more cream, 1/2 teaspoon at a time, to help the dough come together. Form the dough into a disk, wrap in plastic wrap, and refrigerate for at least 4 hours, or overnight.

When ready to bake, preheat the oven to 350°F and line the baking sheets with parchment paper.

On a lightly floured surface using a lightly floured rolling pin, roll the dough to 1/4-inch thickness. Use a cutter to cut shapes and place the cookies 2 inches apart on the prepared baking sheets. Repeat with the remaining dough, gathering up the scraps, re-rolling and cutting until all the dough is used. Bake until golden brown, about 12 to 20 minutes. If you notice butter bubbling up during the baking process you can flip the cookies, but it isn't required. Remove the cookies from the oven and cool for 2 minutes before transferring them to a wire rack to cool.

Spiced Orange and Rye Shortbread

During the holiday season, Melissa Lundquist of St. Paul bakes traditional Norwegian cookies, including sandbakkels and fattigman. "I love making cardamom bread every year, and I'm still working on Swedish limpa bread, although I'm not good at that yet," she said. "That's when I thought, 'Why not put those flavors together?'" A key resource was her grandmother's cookbooks. "I don't remember my grandma making rye cookies, and it never occurred to me to put rye flour in a cookie," she said. "But I love it, so I thought, 'Let's see what happens.'"

MAKES 2 DOZEN COOKIES

FOR CANDIED ORANGE PEEL

1 orange

1 cup granulated sugar, plus extra for garnish

FOR COOKIES

1 cup all-purpose flour

1/3 cup dark rye flour

1/8 teaspoon salt

1/4 teaspoon baking powder

1/2 teaspoon ground anise seed (see Note)

1/2 teaspoon ground cardamom

1 tablespoon finely chopped candied orange peel (see Note)

1/2 cup (1 stick) unsalted butter, at room temperature

1/3 cup packed dark brown sugar

3 tablespoons dark molasses

1/2 teaspoon freshly grated orange zest

FOR GLAZE

1 cup powdered sugar

2 tablespoons finely chopped freshly grated orange zest

2 to 4 tablespoons freshly squeezed orange juice

NOTE This dough must be prepared in advance. Anise seed is available in the bulk spices section of many natural foods co-ops and online. Candied orange peel is available in the baking aisle of many supermarkets, but you can also make your own.

TO PREPARE CANDIED ORANGE PEEL: Cut the peels of 1 orange (bitter white pith removed) into strips. Place the orange peels in a medium saucepan and cover with cold water. Over high heat, bring the water to a boil. Remove from the heat, drain the water and rinse the orange peels. Repeat the process two more times. Combine 1 cup water and 1 cup granulated sugar in a medium saucepan over high heat and bring to a boil, stirring until the sugar is dissolved. Add the cooked orange peels, reduce the heat to a gentle simmer and cook until the orange peels are very soft, about 30 to 45 minutes. Remove from the heat and let the orange peels cool in the syrup. When cool, drain and discard the syrup and arrange the candied orange peels on a rimmed baking sheet. Garnish the candied orange peels with granulated sugar and allow them to sit on the counter (preferably in the sunshine) until they're dry, about 24 hours. You will have extra candied orange peels; store in an airtight container in the freezer for up to 2 months.

TO PREPARE COOKIES: In a medium bowl, whisk together the all-purpose flour, dark rye flour, salt, baking powder, anise, cardamom, and candied orange peel, and reserve.

In the bowl of an electric mixer on medium-high speed, beat the butter and brown sugar until light and fluffy, about 2 to 3 minutes. Add the molasses and orange zest and beat until thoroughly combined. Reduce the speed to low, add the flour mixture, and mix until just combined. Form the dough into a disk, wrap in plastic wrap or wax paper, and refrigerate for 1 hour.

When ready to bake, preheat the oven to 375°F and line the baking sheets with parchment paper. Place a wire rack over wax paper or parchment paper.

Remove the plastic wrap or wax paper from the dough and place the dough between 2 sheets of parchment paper. Using a rolling pin, roll the dough to ¼-inch thickness. Use a 2-inch cookie cutter to cut the dough and place the cookies 2 inches apart on the prepared baking sheets. Repeat with the remaining dough, gathering up the scraps, re-rolling and cutting until all the dough is used. Bake for 12 to 14 minutes (12 minutes for a softer, chewier texture; 14 minutes for a crisper, snappier texture). Remove the cookies from the oven and cool for 5 minutes before transferring them to a wire rack to cool completely.

TO PREPARE GLAZE: In a medium bowl, whisk together the powdered sugar and orange zest. Add the orange juice, 1 tablespoon at a time, whisking until the glaze achieves the desired consistency. Drizzle the glaze over the cookies. Allow the glaze to set before serving.

Viennese Wafers with Lemon

Margaret DeHarpporte of Eden Prairie has been baking this recipe for decades. "It's such a goodie that I keep on making it," she said. "People always like them; they always ask for the recipe." Here's why: "It's basically butter and sugar, so it's nice in the mouth, so thin and crisp," she said. "It's also so simple. I like it that people can't quite put their taste buds on the thyme. It's unexpected, and I get a kick out of that." DeHarpporte is one of those bakers who is always tinkering in her kitchen. "I like to experiment," she said. "I was making muffins with lemon and thyme, and I wondered how those flavors would go with this cookie."

MAKES 2 DOZEN COOKIES

1/2 cup (1 stick) unsalted butter, at room temperature

1/3 cup granulated sugar

1/4 teaspoon vanilla extract

Freshly grated zest from 1 lemon

2 teaspoons freshly chopped thyme, or 1 teaspoon dried thyme

3/4 cup plus 1 tablespoon flour, plus extra for rolling dough

1 egg white, slightly beaten

3/4 cup sliced almonds, roughly chopped

NOTE This dough must be prepared in advance. You can substitute pecans or walnuts for the almonds if you prefer.

In the bowl of an electric mixer on medium-high speed, beat the butter until creamy, about 1 minute. Add the granulated sugar and beat until light and fluffy, about 2 minutes. Add the vanilla extract, lemon zest, and thyme, and beat until thoroughly combined. Reduce the speed to low, add the flour, and mix until just combined. Form the dough into a disk, wrap in plastic wrap, and refrigerate for at least 1 hour, or overnight.

When ready to bake, preheat the oven to 350°F and line the baking sheets with parchment paper.

On a lightly floured surface using a lightly floured rolling pin, roll the dough into a rectangular shape no less than 1/4-inch thick. Trim the edges with a knife or pizza cutter and cut the dough into 1 1/2- to 2-inch squares.

Using a pastry brush, brush the top of the wafers lightly with the egg white and sprinkle with the chopped almonds. Gently press the almonds into the dough. Using a thin-bladed spatula, carefully transfer the wafers to the prepared baking sheets, spacing cookies 1 inch apart. Bake until lightly browned, about 20 minutes. Remove the cookies from the oven and cool for 2 minutes before transferring them to a wire rack to cool completely.

Zazvorniky

When Kevin Hurbanis of Minneapolis was growing up, Zazvorniky were a mainstay of his Slovakian grandmother's delicious Christmas Eve cookie platter. The cookie with the tongue-twisting name (it's pronounced ZAHZ-vor-ni-kee) is now a cherished family tradition that the stay-at-home dad shares with his two children, Jack and Emma. For as long as he can remember, Hurbanis has been making the soft, ginger cookie using the same notched rectangular cookie cutter, although most any cookie cutter will do. Along with the recipe, that special cutter is a treasured memento from his grandmother's kitchen. "It's a nice connection that I have to her," he said, "and an especially nice one that I can share with my kids."

MAKES 3 DOZEN COOKIES

2 1/2 cups flour, plus extra for rolling dough

2 teaspoons ground ginger

1 tablespoon baking powder

2 eggs

2 egg yolks

4 tablespoons (1/2 stick) unsalted butter,
   at room temperature

2 cups powdered sugar

NOTE This dough must be prepared in advance. Use a cookie cutter no wider than 2 inches—otherwise the end results are too puffy.

Line the baking sheets with parchment paper. In a medium bowl, whisk together the flour, ginger, and baking powder, and reserve. In the bowl of an electric mixer on medium-high speed, beat the eggs, egg yolks, and butter until creamy, about 2 minutes. Add the powdered sugar and beat until thoroughly combined. Reduce the speed to low, add the flour mixture, and mix until just combined.

On a lightly floured surface with lightly floured hands, knead the dough well, adding flour if the dough is sticky. Transfer the dough to a large bowl, cover the bowl with plastic wrap, and refrigerate for at least 1 hour.

On a lightly floured surface using a lightly floured rolling pin, roll the dough to 1/2-inch thickness. Using a cookie cutter, cut the dough and place the cookies 1 inch apart on the prepared baking sheets. Repeat with the remaining dough, gathering up the scraps, re-rolling, and cutting until all the dough is used. Cover the baking sheets with plastic wrap and refrigerate overnight.

When ready to bake, preheat the oven to 350°F and remove the plastic wrap from the baking sheets.

Bake for 10 to 12 minutes; the cookies should double in height while baking, with the top half spongier than the bottom. Remove the cookies from the oven and cool for 2 minutes before transferring them to a wire rack to cool completely.

CHAPTER FOUR

Refrigerator Cookies

Almond Palmiers

A last-minute need to fill out a holiday cookie platter found Kay Lieberherr of St. Paul turning to the palmiers at Surdyk's in Minneapolis. "It turned out that everyone asked for the recipe for the palmiers, and not for the cookies that I had baked," she said with a laugh. That response sent her on a mission to develop her own palmier recipe. Using commercially prepared puff pastry makes this recipe a snap to prepare. "I love it when you don't spend a lot of time on something, yet people think, 'Wow, that must have taken days,'" said Lieberherr.

MAKES 2 TO 3 DOZEN COOKIES

4 tablespoons (1/2 stick) unsalted butter, at room temperature

1/4 cup powdered sugar, plus extra for garnish, optional

1 (7-ounce) tube almond paste, cut into small pieces

1 egg

1/2 teaspoon almond extract

1/4 cup granulated sugar, divided

1 (17.3-ounce) package puff pastry sheets, thawed in the refrigerator (see Note)

NOTE This dough must be prepared in advance. Palmiers (pronounced pahlm-YAYs) go by many other names, including elephant ears, palm leaves, and French hearts. Widely available Pepperidge Farm puff pastry works perfectly well with this cookie, but we loved the results from Dufour Pastry Kitchens puff pastry. The all-butter product makes a gloriously light, golden, and flaky palmier.

In the bowl of an electric mixer on medium-high speed, beat the butter until creamy, about 1 minute. Add the powdered sugar and almond paste. Beat until creamy, about 1 minute. Add the egg and almond extract, and beat until thoroughly combined.

Sprinkle a surface with 1 tablespoon granulated sugar. Carefully unfold 1 puff pastry sheet over the granulated sugar and sprinkle with 1 tablespoon granulated sugar.

Using a rolling pin, roll the puff pastry sheet into a 12-inch square. Divide the almond paste mixture in half, and carefully spread half the mixture evenly over the top of the puff pastry sheet. Carefully roll up opposite sides of the puff pastry sheet, from the outer edge to the middle, with the rolls meeting in the center. Firmly press together, wrap the puff pastry roll in plastic wrap, and refrigerate for at least 2 hours, or up to 2 days. Repeat with the second puff pastry sheet.

When ready to bake, preheat the oven to 400°F and line the baking sheets with parchment paper.

Unwrap the puff pastry rolls and, using a sharp knife, trim off the uneven ends. Cut the rolls into 1/4-inch slices and place (flat side down) 2 inches apart on the prepared baking sheets. Bake until golden brown, 12 to 14 minutes. Remove the cookies from the oven and cool for 2 minutes before transferring them to a wire rack to cool completely. Dust with powdered sugar (optional).

Cappuccino Flats

Dianne Sivald of White Bear Lake discovered Cappuccino Flats in a *Better Homes and Gardens* cookbook and adapted these elegant, richly flavored cookies from the original recipe. "They're so good that I wonder why I make them only at Christmas," she said. "But maybe that's what makes them special. You have to wait for them."

MAKES 4 DOZEN COOKIES

FOR COOKIES

2 cups flour
1 teaspoon ground cinnamon
¼ teaspoon salt
2 ounces unsweetened chocolate
1 tablespoon instant espresso powder
1 cup (2 sticks) unsalted butter, at room temperature
½ cup granulated sugar
½ cup packed light brown sugar
1 egg

FOR ICING

1 ½ cups semisweet chocolate pieces
3 tablespoons shortening

NOTE This dough must be prepared in advance. To prepare a gluten-free version, substitute with a ratio of ¾ cup gluten-free flour for 1 cup all-purpose flour.

TO PREPARE COOKIES: In a medium bowl, whisk together the flour, cinnamon, and salt, and reserve.

In a double boiler over gently simmering water (or in a bowl in a microwave oven), melt the unsweetened chocolate, whisking occasionally until smooth. Remove from the heat and cool slightly.

In a small bowl, combine the espresso powder and 1 teaspoon water, and stir until dissolved. In the bowl of an electric mixer on medium-high speed, beat the butter until creamy, about 1 minute. Add the granulated sugar and brown sugar, and beat until light and fluffy, about 2 minutes. Add the melted

chocolate, espresso mixture, and egg, and beat until thoroughly combined. Reduce the speed to low, add the flour mixture, and mix until just combined. Cover the bowl with plastic wrap and refrigerate for at least 1 hour.

Divide the dough into two equal pieces. Form the dough into logs measuring about 7 inches in length and 1 inch in diameter. Wrap the dough logs in plastic wrap and refrigerate for at least 6 hours, or overnight.

When ready to bake, preheat the oven to 350°F and line the baking sheets with parchment paper.

Unwrap the dough and, using a sharp knife, trim off the uneven ends. Cut the dough into ¼-inch slices and place 1 inch apart on the prepared baking sheets. Bake until the edges are firm and lightly browned, about 10 to 12 minutes. Remove the cookies from the oven and cool for 2 minutes before transferring them to a wire rack to cool completely.

TO PREPARE ICING: In a double boiler over gently simmering water (or in a bowl in a microwave oven), combine the semisweet chocolate and shortening, whisking occasionally until smooth. Remove from the heat and let the chocolate mixture cool for a few minutes. Dip one half of each cookie into the chocolate mixture, sliding the back of the cookie on the edge of the pan to remove excess chocolate. Place the cookies on wax paper until the chocolate sets.

Cinnamon Bun Cookies

Patrice Hurd of Bemidji created a cookie that looks and tastes like a cinnamon bun, one that blossomed out of her Finnish grandmother's reputation as "queen of the cinnamon bun." "You walked into her house and the countertops and table were covered with them," Hurd said. "She baked. She shared. It was a communal experience."

MAKES 3 TO 4 DOZEN COOKIES

FOR COOKIES

3 cups flour

1 teaspoon baking powder

1 teaspoon baking soda

1/2 teaspoon salt

1/2 cup (1 stick) unsalted butter, at room temperature

2 tablespoons (1 ounce) cream cheese, at room temperature

1 cup powdered sugar

1 egg

2 teaspoons vanilla extract

FOR FILLING

6 tablespoons (3/4 stick) unsalted butter, at room temperature

3/4 cup packed dark brown sugar

1 tablespoon ground cinnamon (see Note)

1/8 teaspoon salt

FOR ICING

6 tablespoons (3/4 stick) unsalted butter, at room temperature

1/4 cup (2 ounces) cream cheese, at room temperature

Pinch of salt

1/2 teaspoon vanilla extract

1/4 teaspoon almond extract

2 cups powdered sugar

NOTE This dough must be prepared in advance.

TO PREPARE COOKIES: In a medium bowl, whisk together the flour, baking powder, baking soda, and salt, and reserve. In the bowl of an electric mixer on medium-high speed, beat the butter and cream cheese until creamy, about 1 minute. Reduce the speed to low, add the powdered sugar, and mix until combined, about 1 minute. Increase the speed to medium-high and beat until light and fluffy, about 2 minutes. Add the egg and vanilla extract, and mix until thoroughly combined. Reduce the speed to low, add the flour mixture, and mix until just combined and a smooth dough is formed. Divide the dough into 2 equal pieces. Form the dough into disks, wrap in plastic wrap, and refrigerate while preparing the filling.

TO PREPARE FILLING: In the bowl of an electric mixer on medium speed, beat the butter, brown sugar, cinnamon, and salt until smooth. Remove one dough disk and place between two large pieces of parchment or wax paper. Roll the dough to a 9- by 12-inch rectangle (lifting the top piece of the paper and piecing/re-rolling the dough as necessary); then remove the top paper. Dot teaspoon-size pieces of the filling over half of the dough (using half of the filling), and use the back of a spoon to evenly spread the filling across the top of the dough.

Beginning with one long edge, gently roll up the dough, peeling away the bottom layer of parchment or wax paper and taking care not to allow cracks in the dough to appear. Place the dough seam-side down (and gently stretch from the center outward to form a 12-inch long roll, if necessary). Using a sharp knife, cut the roll in half. Wrap the dough rolls in plastic wrap and refrigerate for at least 2 hours, or overnight. Repeat with the remaining dough disk and filling.

When ready to bake, preheat the oven to 375°F and line the baking sheets with parchment paper.

Unwrap the dough rolls and, using a sharp knife, trim off the uneven ends. Cut the dough into ¼-inch slices and place the cookies 2 inches apart on the prepared baking sheets. Bake until the cookies are just set and the edges barely begin to brown, about 8 to 9 minutes. Remove the cookies from the oven and cool for 2 minutes before transferring them to a wire rack to cool completely.

TO PREPARE ICING: While the cookies are in the oven, combine the butter, cream cheese, salt, vanilla extract, and almond extract in the bowl of an electric mixer on medium-high speed. Beat until creamy, about 1 minute. Reduce the speed to low, add the powdered sugar, and mix until smooth.

When the cookies are still warm, top each cookie with about 1 ½ teaspoons icing, and gently spread the icing on the cookies (or fill a pastry bag fitted with a small tip and pipe the icing over the cookies). Cool the cookies completely; then refrigerate until the icing sets. Store the cookies in a tightly covered container in the refrigerator, and serve at room temperature.

Cranberry Lemon Drops

The recipe is a cross between two cookies that Janet Heirigs of Minneapolis has been baking for years. The base is a glazed lemon cookie from *Cook's Illustrated* magazine, and the embellishments were inspired by a Martha Stewart biscotti, one that puts cranberries and pecans front and center. Heirigs often enlists her colleagues in the taste-testing process. For this cookie, she also turned to a group of nuns at a Franciscan retreat she attends several times a year in rural Minnesota. They weren't impressed with a time-consuming cranberry flourish, and Heirigs dropped it. "Then again, they have a 'living simply' belief," she said with a laugh. Our judges remained impressed. "So pretty," said one. "This is what a holiday cookie looks like," added another.

MAKES 3 DOZEN COOKIES

FOR COOKIES

1 3/4 cups flour

1/4 teaspoon salt

1/4 teaspoon baking powder

3/4 cup (1 1/2 sticks) unsalted butter, at room temperature

3/4 cup granulated sugar

1 egg yolk

Freshly grated zest from 2 large lemons

2 tablespoons freshly squeezed lemon juice

1/2 teaspoon vanilla extract

1/2 cup dried cranberries

1/2 cup pecans, toasted (see Note)

FOR ICING

1 tablespoon cream cheese, at room temperature

1 tablespoon unsalted butter, at room temperature

1 to 2 tablespoons freshly squeezed lemon juice

1 1/2 cups powdered sugar

1/4 teaspoon vanilla extract

Freshly grated zest from 1 large lemon

Dried cranberries

15 lemon drop candies, crushed

NOTE This dough must be prepared in advance. To toast pecans, place the nuts in a dry skillet over medium heat, and cook, stirring or shaking the pan frequently, until they just begin to release their fragrance, about 3 to 4 minutes (alternately, preheat oven to 325°F, spread the nuts on an ungreased baking sheet, and bake, stirring often, for 4 to 6 minutes). Remove the nuts from the heat and cool to room temperature. For easier cleanup after crushing the lemon drop candies, consider placing candies in a paper or plastic bag, or line the top of a cutting board with parchment paper or wax paper, and cover the candy with the same.

TO PREPARE COOKIES: In a medium bowl, whisk together the flour, salt, and baking powder, and reserve.

In the bowl of an electric mixer on medium-high speed, beat the butter until creamy, about 1 minute. Add the granulated sugar and beat until light and fluffy, about 2 minutes. Add the egg yolk, lemon zest, lemon juice, and vanilla extract, and beat until thoroughly combined. Reduce the speed to low, add the flour mixture, and mix until just combined. Stir in the dried cranberries and pecans. Divide the dough into two equal pieces. Roll the dough into logs measuring 1 1/2-inches in diameter. Wrap the dough logs in plastic wrap and refrigerate for at least 2 hours.

When ready to bake, preheat the oven to 375°F and line the baking sheets with parchment paper.

Unwrap the dough logs and, using a sharp knife, trim off the uneven ends. Cut the dough into ⅜-inch slices and place 1 inch apart on prepared baking sheets. Bake until the centers of the cookies begin to color and the edges are a light golden brown, about 13 to 16 minutes. Remove the cookies from the oven and cool for 2 minutes before transferring them to a wire rack to cool completely.

TO PREPARE ICING: In the bowl of an electric mixer on medium speed, combine the cream cheese, butter, lemon juice, powdered sugar, vanilla extract, and lemon zest, and mix until smooth. Spread the icing with a knife or a piping bag fitted with a small tip. Top with dried cranberries, and sprinkle the tops of the cookies with crushed lemon drops.

Cranberry Pecan Swirls

"We're okay with chocolate, but our family thing is cranberries—we love them," said Annette Poole of Prior Lake, who proceeded to detail an impressive list of favorite sauces, pies, and cakes that put the scarlet berry in the spotlight. "I could be their spokesperson." While on a vacation, Poole stumbled across this recipe in a book, and it grabbed her eye. "I like the pictures; that's what sells it for me," she said. "If I see something that appeals to me visually, then I'll make it." She made a copy and set it aside. Fast-forward a few years. She finally baked it, and flipped over it. "One of the reasons I like it is because it's not too sweet; there's not a lot of sugar in the filling," she said. "And yes, the fresh cranberries. I'm always on the lookout for anything cranberry. If there's a cranberry recipe, I've got to have it."

MAKES 3 DOZEN COOKIES

FOR COOKIES

1 ½ cups flour, plus extra for rolling dough

¼ teaspoon baking powder

¼ teaspoon salt

½ cup (1 stick) unsalted butter, at room temperature

¾ cup granulated sugar

1 egg

1 teaspoon vanilla extract

FOR FILLING

⅓ cup finely chopped fresh cranberries

½ cup ground pecans

1 tablespoon freshly grated orange zest

NOTE This dough must be prepared in advance.

TO PREPARE COOKIES: In a medium bowl, whisk together the flour, baking powder, and salt, and reserve. In the bowl of an electric mixer on medium-high speed, beat the butter and granulated sugar until light and fluffy, about 2 minutes. Add the egg and vanilla extract, and beat until thoroughly combined. Reduce the speed to low, add the flour mixture, and mix until just combined. Cover the bowl with plastic wrap and refrigerate for at least 1 hour.

TO PREPARE FILLING: In a small bowl, combine the cranberries, pecans, and orange zest.

TO ASSEMBLE COOKIES: On a lightly floured surface using a lightly floured rolling pin, roll the dough to a 10-inch square. Sprinkle the cranberry mixture over the dough, leaving a ½-inch border on two opposite sides. Roll the dough, jelly-roll fashion, beginning at one of the borders and rolling toward the other border. Wrap the dough in plastic wrap and freeze for at least 8 hours.

When ready to bake, preheat the oven to 375°F and line the baking sheets with parchment paper.

Unwrap the dough and, using a sharp knife, trim off the uneven ends. Cut the dough into ¼-inch thick slices and place 2 inches apart on the prepared baking sheets. Bake until lightly browned, 14 to 15 minutes. Remove the cookies from the oven and cool for 2 minutes before transferring them to a wire rack to cool completely.

Korova Cookies

Always in the mood for anything chocolate, Mary Eckmeier of St. Paul plucked this recipe from *Paris Sweets* by Dorie Greenspan and then stamped it with her own imprint. "The author said to cut up chocolate, but chips are so much easier," she said. While the original recipe calls for coarse sea salt, Eckmeier gets a little more specific and uses *sel de guérande,* harvested from the salt marshes of Brittany in France.

MAKES 3 DOZEN COOKIES

1 ¼ cups flour

⅓ cup unsweetened cocoa powder

½ teaspoon *sel de guérande* or other coarse
  sea salt (see Note)

½ teaspoon baking soda

½ cup plus 3 tablespoons (1 stick plus
  3 tablespoons) unsalted butter, at room
  temperature

⅔ cup packed light brown sugar

¼ cup granulated sugar

1 teaspoon vanilla extract

5 ounces (about ¾ cup) semisweet
  chocolate chips

NOTE This dough must be prepared in advance. Sea salt places an unexpectedly glamorous gloss on humble slice-and-bake refrigerator cookies. This recipe calls specifically for *sel de guérande*, a gray sea salt harvested from the salt marshes of Brittany that is available at many specialty cooking stores. That little bit of crunchy French sea salt makes the cookie feel not quite so sweet. Feel free to substitute other sea salts.

In a medium bowl, whisk together the flour, cocoa powder, sea salt, and baking soda, and reserve. In the bowl of an electric mixer on medium-high speed, beat the butter until creamy, about 1 minute. Add the brown sugar, granulated sugar, and vanilla extract, and beat until light and fluffy, about 2 minutes. Reduce the speed to low, add the flour mixture, and mix until a moist, crumbly dough forms. Fold in the chocolate chips.

On a clean surface, knead the dough a few times to finish mixing (the warmth of your hands will help the mixture come together). Divide the dough into two equal pieces. Form the dough into logs measuring about 1 ½ inches in diameter. Wrap the dough logs in plastic wrap and refrigerate for at least 3 hours, or up to 3 days.

When ready to bake, preheat the oven to 325°F and line the baking sheets with parchment paper.

Unwrap the dough logs and, using a sharp knife, trim off the uneven ends. Cut the dough into ½-inch slices (if the cookies come apart after slicing, just push the dough back together using your fingers) and place 2 inches apart on the prepared baking sheets. Bake 12 minutes. Remove the cookies from the oven and cool 5 minutes before transferring them to a wire rack to cool completely.

Marzipan Cherry Shortbread

For Cynthia Baxter, inspiration for this easy-to-prepare cookie came from several sources, starting with Moose & Sadie's, a cafe formerly in her Minneapolis neighborhood, where scones with marzipan and tart cherries were an occasional bakery star. "I got to thinking that those flavors would make a great cookie," she said. The semolina came from a recipe that her husband loved, and the shortbread format was a given. "It's my favorite kind of cookie," she said. "I wanted to have a roll of dough that you could keep in the freezer, and cut it when you wanted more cookies. I found a basic shortbread recipe, then I adapted it."

MAKES 2 DOZEN COOKIES

1 cup all-purpose flour
1/2 cup semolina flour
1/4 teaspoon salt
1/2 cup (1 stick) unsalted butter, at room temperature
1/4 cup marzipan (about 3 1/2 ounces, or 1/2 tube), at room temperature, cut into small pieces (see Note)
1/3 cup packed light brown sugar
1/4 teaspoon vanilla extract
1 tablespoon milk, plus more if necessary
1/4 cup chopped blanched slivered almonds
1/2 cup chopped dried cherries
1 egg white
1/4 cup turbinado sugar (or granulated sugar, or a decorative sugar, see Note)

NOTE This dough must be prepared in advance. Almond paste can be substituted for marzipan. Turbinado sugar is a caramel-colored crystal sugar.

In a medium bowl, whisk together the all-purpose flour, semolina flour, and salt, and reserve.

In the bowl of an electric mixer on medium-high speed, beat the butter, marzipan (or almond paste), and brown sugar until light and fluffy, about 2 minutes. Add the vanilla extract and 1 tablespoon milk and beat until thoroughly combined. Reduce the speed to low.

Add the flour mixture in three additions, mixing until just combined (if the dough is too crumbly, add additional milk, 1 teaspoon at a time and up to 1 tablespoon, until a dough forms). Stir in the almonds and dried cherries.

Form the dough into a log measuring about 12 inches in length and 1 1/2 inches in diameter. Wrap the dough log in plastic wrap and refrigerate for at least 2 hours.

When ready to bake, preheat the oven to 325°F and line the baking sheets with parchment paper.

In a small bowl, whisk the egg white and 1 tablespoon water until slightly foamy. Brush the dough log with the egg white mixture. Roll the dough log in turbinado sugar (or granulated sugar, or a decorative sugar) to coat the surface. Using a sharp knife, trim off the uneven ends. Slice the dough into 1/4-inch cookies and place 2 inches apart on the prepared baking sheets. Bake until the bottoms are lightly browned, about 18 to 22 minutes. Remove the cookies from the oven and cool for 2 minutes before transferring them to a wire rack to cool completely.

Nancy's Anise Pecan Cookies

Mary Jane Nickerson of Montevideo is a cookie fan. "They're not like cake," she said. "You can have a little cookie, or two, and not feel guilty." She came by this recipe through a friend. "Nancy Harrington lives in New Bedford, Massachusetts, and when we lived near there, I used to get cookies every Christmas from her," Nickerson said. "These were the best ones. I rummaged through the tin every year and ate them first. I finally asked her for the recipe. Nancy thinks this might be a Pillsbury recipe from the 1940s or 1950s that she altered. She's always taking liberties with recipes, making them better." Anise is the attention-grabber: "It's a different flavor from your regular Christmas cookies," Nickerson said. "It's a surprise, you know?"

MAKES 4 DOZEN COOKIES

2 1/2 cups flour

1 teaspoon baking soda

1/2 teaspoon salt

1/2 teaspoon ground cloves

1/2 teaspoon ground cinnamon

1 tablespoon anise seeds

1 cup (2 sticks) unsalted butter, at room temperature

1 cup granulated sugar

1 cup packed light brown sugar

2 eggs

1/2 cup finely chopped pecans

NOTE This dough must be prepared in advance.

In a medium bowl, whisk together the flour, baking soda, salt, cloves, cinnamon, and anise seeds, and reserve.

In the bowl of an electric mixer on medium-high speed, beat the butter, granulated sugar, and brown sugar until light and fluffy, about 2 minutes. Add the eggs, one at a time, beating well after each addition. Reduce the speed to low. Add the flour mixture in three additions, mixing until just combined. Stir in the pecans.

Divide the dough into two equal pieces. Form the dough into two logs, each measuring about 10 inches long. Wrap the dough logs in wax paper and refrigerate for at least 4 hours, or overnight.

When ready to bake, preheat the oven to 350°F and line the baking sheets with parchment paper.

Unwrap the dough logs and, using a sharp knife, trim off the uneven ends. Cut the dough into 1/4-inch slices and place 2 inches apart on the prepared baking sheets. Bake for 9 to 10 minutes. Remove the cookies from the oven and cool for 2 minutes before transferring them to a wire rack to cool completely.

New Scenic Cookies

During a visit to the New Scenic Cafe along the North Shore near Duluth, Gwen Gold-smith of Minneapolis ordered one of the restaurant's signature dishes that features figs, maple brown butter, walnuts, and blue cheese. "I got this notion that these flavors would turn into a cookie," she said. The dough is based on a maple-flavored cookie from *Fine Cooking* magazine's website, then Goldsmith's creativity took over. "I'm flattered," said Scott Graden, the restaurant's chef and owner. "You've got me smiling, and now I want the recipe. Or at least a batch of cookies."

MAKES 2 1/2 DOZEN COOKIES

FOR BROWN BUTTER

3/4 cup (1 1/2 sticks) unsalted butter

FOR COOKIES

2 1/2 cups flour

1/2 teaspoon salt

1/4 teaspoon baking soda

3/4 cup granulated sugar

1/4 cup packed dark brown sugar

1 1/2 teaspoons maple extract

1 egg

1/4 cup maple syrup

1 teaspoon vanilla extract

1 cup chopped walnuts, toasted (see Note)

1 cup fig preserves

4 ounces (or more) blue cheese, crumbled

NOTE This dough must be prepared in advance. To toast walnuts, place the nuts in a dry skillet over medium heat and cook, stirring (or shaking the pan frequently), until they just begin to release their fragrance, about 3 to 4 minutes (alternatively, preheat the oven to 325°F, spread the nuts on an ungreased baking sheet and bake, stirring often, for 4 to 6 minutes).

TO PREPARE BROWN BUTTER: In a medium saucepan over medium heat, melt the butter, stirring constantly, until it smells nutty and browned bits begin to form at the bottom of the pan, about 5 minutes. Remove from the heat, transfer the brown butter to a small bowl, and reserve.

TO PREPARE COOKIES: In a medium bowl, whisk together the flour, salt, and baking soda, and reserve.

In the bowl of an electric mixer on low speed, combine the granulated sugar, brown sugar, and maple extract, and mix until thoroughly combined. Add the cooled brown butter, and mix until thoroughly combined. Add the egg, maple syrup, and vanilla extract, and mix until thoroughly combined. Add the flour mixture until just combined.

Form the dough into a log, wrap in plastic wrap, and refrigerate for at least 1 hour.

When the dough is firm, remove and discard the plastic wrap and place the dough between layers of parchment paper. Using a rolling pin, roll the dough into a rectangle about 5 inches wide, 20 inches long, and 1/4-inch thick. For ease in working with it, cut the dough in half the short way to make 2 (10-inch) rectangles.

Spread half of the fig preserves evenly in a thin layer over each 10-inch rectangle, leaving a 1/2-inch border along the long edges. Sprinkle the walnuts over the fig preserves, then sprinkle the crumbled blue cheese.

Starting at the long end, carefully roll each of the rectangles into a log, using the parchment paper to help the process. Lightly press the long end of each log to form a seam, discarding the parchment paper.

Wrap the dough logs in plastic wrap and refrigerate for at least 2 hours. (At this point, the dough can be wrapped in aluminum foil and frozen, for up to 1 month; thaw overnight in the refrigerator before baking.)

When ready to bake, preheat the oven to 350°F and line the baking sheets with parchment paper.

Unwrap the dough logs. Using a thin serrated knife, cut ¼-inch to ⅓-inch thick cookies and place 2 inches apart on the prepared baking sheets. Bake until the edges are lightly browned, about 18 minutes. Remove the cookies from the oven and cool for 2 minutes before transferring them to a wire rack to cool completely.

Orange Turmeric Cookies

December is a busy month for Kathy Valentine of Plymouth. "Every year, I make tons of Christmas cookies," she said. "Baking cookies, that's my passion." Entering the contest was Valentine's sister's idea. "I've always wanted to, but I never did, because you have to figure out a cookie that's different," said Valentine. "Turmeric is trendy, so I Googled 'turmeric cookies,' and I found this recipe and thought, 'You have to try that.' It's not too sweet, and it's a little bit savory. It has complex flavors."

MAKES 3 DOZEN COOKIES

FOR COOKIES

2 cups flour

3/4 cup powdered sugar

1/4 teaspoon baking powder

1/4 teaspoon salt

1 tablespoon freshly grated orange zest

1/2 teaspoon ground ginger

1/2 teaspoon turmeric

3/4 cup (1 1/2 sticks) cold unsalted butter, cut into tablespoon-size pieces

2 tablespoons freshly squeezed orange juice, plus extra if needed

1 teaspoon vanilla extract

FOR GLAZE

3/4 cup powdered sugar

1/4 to 1/2 teaspoon ground ginger

1/4 to 1/2 teaspoon turmeric

1 to 2 tablespoons freshly squeezed orange juice

About 3 tablespoons large-crystal decorative sugar

NOTE This dough must be prepared in advance. The recipe originated in *The Good Cookie* by Tish Boyle and was adapted by Wendy Sondov of themondaybox.com.

TO PREPARE COOKIES: In the bowl of an electric mixer on low speed, combine the flour, powdered sugar, baking powder, salt, orange zest, ginger, and turmeric. Add the butter, increase the speed to medium and mix until the butter is in small pieces throughout the flour mixture (alternately, in a food processor fitted with a metal blade, pulse together the flour, powdered sugar, baking powder, salt, orange zest, ginger, and turmeric. Add the butter and pulse until the butter is in small pieces throughout the flour mixture).

In a small bowl, stir together the 2 tablespoons orange juice and vanilla extract. Add the orange juice mixture to the flour mixture and mix just until a dough forms (or, if using a food processor, pour the orange juice mixture into the dough and pulse just until a dough forms). You may need to add more juice, 1/2 teaspoon at a time, to help the dough come together.

Form the dough into a log measuring about 10 inches in length. Wrap the dough log in plastic wrap and refrigerate for at least 2 hours.

When ready to bake, preheat the oven to 325°F and line the baking sheets with parchment paper. Place a wire rack over wax paper or parchment paper.

Unwrap the dough. Using a sharp, thin-bladed knife, slice the dough into 1/4-inch thick cookies and place 1 inch apart on the prepared baking sheets. Bake until the bottom edges begin to turn golden, about 12 to 15 minutes; the surface should not brown. Remove the cookies from the oven and cool for 2 minutes before transferring them to a wire rack to cool completely.

TO PREPARE GLAZE: In a small bowl, combine the powdered sugar, ginger, and turmeric. Add the orange juice, ½ tablespoon at a time, mixing until a drizzling/spreading consistency is achieved. Spread the glaze over a few cookies at a time, then immediately sprinkle with decorative sugar. Repeat with the remaining cookies. Allow the glaze to set before serving.

Pistachio Pine Cones

"I love pistachios," said Linda McEwen of Mahtomedi. "It's fun that they're green—that fits with Christmas." She found this recipe in *Midwest Living* magazine.

MAKES 4 DOZEN COOKIES

FOR COOKIES

1 cup (2 sticks) unsalted butter, at room temperature

¾ cup granulated sugar

½ teaspoon vanilla extract

¼ teaspoon salt

1 vanilla bean

2 cups flour

2 cups finely chopped salted, dry-roasted pistachios, shelled and divided (see Note)

FOR COATING

12 ounces white chocolate

1 tablespoon shortening

NOTE This dough must be prepared in advance. If salted, dry-roasted pistachios are unavailable, toast and salt them yourself. Place nuts in a dry skillet over medium heat, sprinkle with ½ teaspoon salt, and cook, stirring or shaking the pan frequently, until they just begin to release their fragrance, about 2 to 3 minutes (or preheat oven to 325°F, spread nuts on an ungreased baking sheet, sprinkle with ½ teaspoon salt, and bake, stirring often, for 4 to 6 minutes). Remove the nuts from the heat and cool to room temperature. Chop all the nuts before beginning the recipe. This recipe works well when substituting gluten-free flour for all-purpose flour.

TO PREPARE COOKIES: In the bowl of an electric mixer on medium-high speed, beat the butter for 1 minute. Add the granulated sugar, vanilla extract, and salt, and beat until just combined. Split the vanilla bean in half lengthwise. Using the tip of a paring knife, scrape the seeds from the bean into the butter mixture, and beat until thoroughly combined. Reduce the speed to low, add the flour in ½-cup increments, and mix just until combined. Stir in 1 cup of the pistachios.

Divide the dough into two equal pieces. Form the dough into logs measuring 1 ½-inches in diameter, giving the log an oval shape (one with distinctive wider and narrower ends) so that the cut cookies will resemble a pine cone shape. Wrap the dough logs in plastic wrap and refrigerate for at least 2 hours, or up to 2 days.

When ready to bake, preheat the oven to 375°F and line the baking sheets with parchment paper.

Unwrap the dough logs and, using a sharp knife, trim off the uneven ends. Cut the dough into ¼-inch slices and place 1 inch apart on the prepared baking sheets. Bake until just firm and browned on the bottoms, about 10 to 12 minutes. Remove the cookies from the oven and cool for 2 minutes before transferring them to a wire rack to cool completely.

TO PREPARE COATING: In a double boiler over gently simmering water (or in a bowl in a microwave oven), combine the white chocolate and shortening, whisking occasionally until smooth. Place the remaining 1 cup of chopped pistachios in a wide bowl. Dip the wider end of each cookie in the melted white chocolate (to resemble a pine cone), then dip in the pistachios. Transfer the cookies to wax paper and let stand until set.

Swedish Shortbread Cookies

Even though the recipe didn't originate with her, Marsha Morrissette's friends and family know that Swedish Shortbread Cookies are synonymous with her and the yuletide season. "It's the only Christmas cookie I make," said the Eden Prairie resident. "Everyone loves them, so why make anything else?" She first encountered the buttery treat at a cookie exchange, and it was love at first almond-and-raspberry bite. Her friend graciously shared the recipe, and a family holiday tradition—and a contest finalist—was born. Over the years, Morrissette learned to prepare the simple beauties no earlier than a week in advance—not for reasons of freshness, but because they disappear. "They're even good when you steal them straight out of the freezer," she said. "No defrosting necessary."

MAKES 3 DOZEN COOKIES

1 cup (2 sticks) unsalted butter, at room
    temperature
¹/₂ cup plus 2 tablespoons granulated sugar
2 to 2 ¹/₃ cups flour
¹/₃ cup raspberry jam
1 cup powdered sugar
1 teaspoon almond extract

NOTE This dough must be prepared in advance.

In the bowl of an electric mixer on medium-high speed, beat the butter and granulated sugar until creamy, about 2 minutes. Reduce the speed to low, add 2 cups flour, and mix until just combined (if dough is sticky, add more flour, 1 tablespoon at a time, up to ¹/₃ cup). Divide the dough into six equal pieces. Form the dough into balls, wrap in plastic wrap, and refrigerate for 30 minutes.

When ready to bake, preheat the oven to 350°F. Place a wire rack over wax paper or parchment paper.

Place a dough ball between two sheets of parchment paper and, using a rolling pin, roll the dough to ¹/₄-inch thickness, forming a 3- by 10-inch rectangle. Carefully peel away the top layer of the parchment paper.

Make a shallow crease down the center of the rectangle and fill the crease with raspberry jam. Carefully transfer the dough, retaining the parchment paper, to a baking sheet. Repeat the process with the remaining dough. Bake until the edges become golden brown, 10 to 12 minutes. Remove the cookies from the oven, cool for 2 minutes, and cut across the short side of the rectangle at a slight angle, making 6 or so cookies. Transfer the cookies to the prepared wire rack to cool completely.

In a small bowl, whisk together the powdered sugar, almond extract, and 2 to 3 teaspoons of water, until smooth. Drizzle the glaze over the cookies. Allow the glaze to set before serving.

CONTENTS

CHAPTER FIVE

Bar Cookies

Almond Ricotta Bars

A lemon ricotta cookie at a favorite Mall of America restaurant sparked the imagination of Karen Cope of Minneapolis. She tried a few versions and liked them, but ultimately decided to streamline the process by going the bar cookie route, adding an icing (her favorite cream cheese–based frosting) and then playing with flavors. "I love almond, and I always have almond extract on hand," she said. "The recipe has the equivalent of a tablespoon of almond extract, and I was a little nervous about putting too much almond in. But then a friend didn't think it was almondy enough." It is.

MAKES 4 DOZEN BARS

FOR BARS

2 ½ cups flour

1 tablespoon baking powder

1 teaspoon salt

1 cup (2 sticks) unsalted butter, at room temperature, plus extra for pan

2 cups granulated sugar

2 eggs

2 teaspoons almond extract

1 teaspoon vanilla extract

15 ounces whole-milk ricotta cheese

FOR FROSTING

½ cup (1 stick) unsalted butter, at room temperature

4 ounces cream cheese, at room temperature

3 cups powdered sugar

1 teaspoon almond extract

½ cup sliced almonds, toasted (see Note)

NOTE To toast almonds, place the nuts in a dry skillet over medium heat and cook, stirring or shaking the pan frequently, until they just begin to release their fragrance, about 3 to 4 minutes (alternately, preheat the oven to 325°F, spread the nuts on an ungreased baking sheet, and bake, stirring often, for 4 to 6 minutes). Remove the nuts from the heat and cool to room temperature. For the best flavor, avoid substitutions with this recipe—use whole-milk ricotta, not low-fat. For more cake-like bars, use a 9- by 13-inch pan.

TO PREPARE BARS: Preheat the oven to 325°F. Butter the bottom and sides of a 13- by 18-inch half-sheet pan.

In a medium bowl, whisk together the flour, baking powder, and salt, and reserve.

In the bowl of an electric mixer on medium-high speed, beat the butter until creamy, about 1 minute. Add the granulated sugar and beat until light and fluffy, about 2 minutes. Add the eggs, one at a time, and beat until thoroughly combined. Add the almond extract and vanilla extract, and beat until thoroughly combined. Reduce the speed to low and add the ricotta in three additions, mixing until just combined. Gradually add the flour mixture until just combined.

Spread the batter in the prepared pan and bake until the cake is set, lightly golden, and the edges are starting to pull away from the sides of the pan, about 35 to 45 minutes. Remove the pan from the oven and place it on a wire rack to cool completely.

TO PREPARE FROSTING: In the bowl of an electric mixer on medium-high speed, beat the butter and cream cheese until light and fluffy, about 2 minutes. Reduce the speed to low, add the powdered sugar and almond extract, and beat until the mixture is uniform and creamy. Spread the frosting over the cooled bar cookies, slice into squares, and top squares with toasted almonds.

Almond Triangles

When a recipe requires four sticks of butter and five cups of almonds, can there possibly be a downside? No. Charlotte Midthun of Granite Falls encountered this recipe in *First for Women* magazine and had a hunch it would be a hit. "I took these to a party, and everyone loved them," she said. "I've been making them ever since. They're such a nice contrast to all the chocolate cookies and sugar cookies at Christmas." They sure are.

MAKES 4 TO 6 DOZEN COOKIES

2 cups (4 sticks) unsalted butter, at room
   temperature, divided
3/4 cup granulated sugar, divided
1 egg
3/4 teaspoon almond extract
1/2 teaspoon salt
2 3/4 cups flour
1 cup packed light brown sugar
1/3 cup honey
1/4 cup heavy cream
1 pound (about 5 1/4 cups) sliced almonds

NOTE This dough must be prepared in advance. These bar cookies freeze really well.

Carefully line a 10- by 15-inch jelly roll pan with aluminum foil, shiny side up.

In the bowl of an electric mixer on medium-high speed, beat 1 cup butter until creamy, about 1 minute. Gradually add 1/2 cup granulated sugar and beat until light and fluffy, about 2 minutes. Add the egg, almond extract, and salt, and beat until thoroughly combined. Reduce the speed to low, add the flour, and mix until just combined. Press the dough evenly into the pan and push the dough up the sides. Cover the pan with plastic wrap and refrigerate for 30 minutes.

When ready to bake, preheat the oven to 375°F.

Using a fork, prick the dough in 20 to 24 places all across the dough and bake 10 minutes. Remove the pan from the oven and place it on a wire rack to cool.

In a large saucepan over medium heat, combine the brown sugar, honey, remaining 1 cup butter, and remaining 1/4 cup granulated sugar, and cook, stirring occasionally, until the sugar dissolves. Increase the heat to medium-high, bring the mixture to a boil, and cook for 3 minutes without stirring.

Remove the pan from the heat and stir in the cream. Stir in the almonds. Spread the almond mixture evenly over the crust. Return the pan to the oven and bake until bubbling, about 15 minutes. Remove the pan from the oven and place on a wire rack to cool. While the bar cookies are still slightly warm, cut them into triangles.

Cardamom Shortbread Cookies

The sorry state of Alecia Enger's recipe card for her Cardamom Shortbread Cookies—stained, splattered, and smudged—is a testament to their popularity. Enger conjured up the bar cookie decades ago, a response to her mother's love of shortbread and Enger's dislike of fussy shortbread molds. "I was pressed for time," said the Hudson, Wisconsin, resident. "So instead of using a mold, I just pressed the dough into a 9- by 13-inch pan." She has made them more times than she can count—with good reason. Not only do they make a lasting impression on eaters, but they are a snap in the kitchen, and the cardamom is a nod to Enger's Scandinavian ancestry.

MAKES 3 DOZEN COOKIES

FOR COOKIES

2 cups flour

2 teaspoons ground cardamom

¼ teaspoon salt

1 cup (2 sticks) unsalted butter, at room temperature

½ cup granulated sugar

½ cup packed light brown sugar

1 egg, separated

1 teaspoon vanilla extract

⅓ cup chopped nuts

FOR ICING

1½ tablespoons unsalted butter, melted

½ teaspoon vanilla extract

1 cup powdered sugar

Milk as needed

Candied fruit for garnish, optional

NOTE These take a longer-than-normal time in the oven—an hour, at a lower-than-normal temperature.

TO PREPARE COOKIES: Preheat the oven to 275°F.

In a medium bowl, whisk together the flour, cardamom, and salt, and reserve.

In the bowl of an electric mixer on medium-high speed, beat the butter until creamy, about 1 minute. Add the granulated sugar and brown sugar, and beat until light and fluffy, about 2 minutes. Add the egg yolk and

vanilla extract, and beat until thoroughly combined. Reduce the speed to low, add the flour mixture, and mix until just combined. Spread the dough into an ungreased 9- by 13-inch baking pan. Brush the reserved egg white over the dough, sprinkle evenly with chopped nuts, and bake for 60 minutes. Remove the pan from the oven and place on a wire rack to cool.

TO PREPARE ICING: In the bowl of an electric mixer on medium speed, beat the melted butter, vanilla extract, and powdered sugar until creamy, about 2 minutes. Add milk, 1 teaspoon at a time, until the icing reaches drizzling consistency. Spread the icing on the slightly warm bars and garnish with the candied fruit (optional). Allow the icing to set. Cut the bar cookies while they are still slightly warm.

Kit-Kat Treats

"It's a super-stupid recipe, but I mean that in the nicest possible way," said Julie Olson of East Bethel. "I love cooking. I can cook like nobody's business. But I'm not a baker. But even if you're not a baker, you can make them, because they're so incredibly easy." Olson gleaned the recipe from her mother-in-law ("It was a collaboration between us," she said), and she's been making the recipe "for forever." Although she prepares Kit-Kat Treats year-round, during the holidays Olson makes them extra-special. "I try to make these festive looking," she said. "Sugars, or sprinkles, or other decorations. You can make them however you'd like."

MAKES 3 DOZEN BARS

1 cup (2 sticks) unsalted butter

1/2 cup milk

1/3 cup granulated sugar

1 cup packed light brown sugar

2 cups crushed graham crackers (about 32 square crackers)

1 (14 ounces) box club crackers

1/2 cup semisweet chocolate chips

1/2 cup butterscotch chips

1/3 cup peanut butter

Decorative sugar and/or chopped dry-roasted, unsalted peanuts, optional

NOTE Decorate with dry-roasted, unsalted peanuts to make obvious to those with food allergies that these no-bake bar cookies contain peanuts. Natural peanut butter (no sugar added) really works well for these bar cookies.

In a saucepan over medium heat, combine the butter, milk, granulated sugar, brown sugar, and graham crackers. Bring to a boil and stir continuously for 5 minutes; do not allow the mixture to burn. Remove the pan from the heat.

Line the bottom of a 9- by 13-inch pan with a single layer of club crackers. Pour half of the graham cracker mixture over the club crackers. Add a second layer of club crackers over the mixture. Pour the remaining half of the graham cracker mixture over the second layer of club crackers. Add a third layer of club crackers. Cover the pan with plastic wrap and refrigerate until set, at least 30 minutes.

When the bars are set, combine the chocolate chips, butterscotch chips, and peanut butter in a double boiler over gently simmering water (or in a bowl in a microwave oven), whisking occasionally until smooth. Pour the melted topping over the top layer of club crackers and spread evenly across the bars. Sprinkle with the decorative sugar and/or peanuts (optional). Allow the chocolate topping to set. Cut into square bar cookies and serve.

Kossuth Kifli

The lemon-infused, walnut-topped, crescent-shaped Kossuth Kifli (pronounced coo-SOOTH KEY-flee) may be the only cookie bearing a general's name. Honoring historical figures with a cookie christening is a time-honored Hungarian tradition, said Linda Paul of Minneapolis. These cutouts (*kifli* is Hungarian for crescent) are a tribute to General Louis Kossuth, a nineteenth-century Hungarian revolutionary hero. Paul's entry originated with her mother's Hungarian church social group cookbook in Detroit. "Most of the recipes listed the ingredients but offered no instructions," Paul said with a laugh. But that culinary roadblock didn't stop this avid baker, and Kossuth Kifli have been at the heart of her holiday baking repertoire for several decades. "People love them," Paul said. "Maybe it's because they look a heck of a lot more difficult to make than they really are."

MAKES 2 TO 3 DOZEN COOKIES

2 teaspoons baking powder

1 ²/₃ cups flour, plus extra for pan

1 cup (2 sticks) unsalted butter, at room
   temperature, plus extra for pan

1 ½ cups granulated sugar

8 eggs, separated

½ teaspoon vanilla extract

Freshly grated zest and juice from 1 lemon

1 ½ cups finely chopped walnuts

Powdered sugar for garnish

Preheat the oven to 350°F. Butter and flour the bottom and sides of a 9- by 13-inch cake pan.

In a medium bowl, whisk together the baking powder and flour, and reserve.

In the bowl of an electric mixer on medium-high speed, beat the butter until creamy, about 1 minute. Add the granulated sugar and beat until light and fluffy, about 2 minutes. Add the egg yolks, one at a time, and beat until creamy. Add the vanilla extract, lemon zest, and lemon juice, and beat until thoroughly combined. Reduce the speed to low, gradually add the flour mixture, and mix until just combined.

In the bowl of an electric mixer fitted with a whisk attachment on medium-high speed, whip the egg whites until they form stiff, glossy (but not dry) peaks. Using a spatula, fold the egg whites into the batter. Gently spread the batter into the prepared pan. Evenly sprinkle the top of the batter with walnuts and bake 25 to 30 minutes. Remove the pan from the oven and place on a wire rack to cool.

Cool until the cake shrinks away from the sides of the pan, about 15 minutes. With a small round biscuit cutter periodically dipped in powdered sugar, cut one circle (don't remove it), then cut another circle halfway down the first one, making two crescents and one oval scrap. Remove from the pan and repeat. Cool the crescents completely. Dust with powdered sugar. Store in a tightly covered container for up to 2 days.

Spumoni Squares

Joanne Holtmeier of Edina has a fanatical attachment to the spumoni ice cream occasionally in the scoop case at Sebastian Joe's in Minneapolis. "I'm a little worried that Sebastian Joe's thinks I'm a stalker," she said. "I'd call, or pop in, just to ask, 'Do you have the spumoni?'" One day, a staffer kindly revealed the ice cream's key ingredients to the flavor's No. 1 fan. "Lemon peel, orange peel, apricots, and almonds," said Holtmeier. "I love those flavors and I thought, 'Hmm, I'm going to bake this into a cookie.'"

MAKES 2 DOZEN BARS

FOR COOKIE BASE

2 1/2 cups flour
1 teaspoon baking powder
1/2 teaspoon salt
3/4 cup (1 1/2 sticks) unsalted butter, at room temperature, plus extra for pan
1 cup granulated sugar
1 egg
1 teaspoon almond extract
1 egg white

FOR TOPPING

1 cup finely chopped dried apricots (see Note)
1 cup chopped walnuts (see Note)
1/2 cup chopped almonds, lightly salted and roasted (see Note)
1/3 cup granulated sugar
1 1/2 teaspoons freshly grated lemon zest
1/2 teaspoon freshly grated orange zest
1/4 teaspoon salt
4 tablespoons (1/2 stick) unsalted butter, at room temperature, cut into small pieces

FOR GLAZE

1/3 cup honey
2 tablespoons unsalted butter
1 tablespoon brown sugar
1/2 teaspoon freshly squeezed lemon juice
1 teaspoon orange liqueur (see Note)

NOTE Use any combination of dried fruits and nuts (pistachios, cashews, cranberries, cherries) as long as you keep the amounts the same. Orange liqueurs include Cointreau,

Grand Marnier, and triple sec. If preferred, substitute freshly squeezed orange juice for orange liqueur.

TO PREPARE COOKIE BASE: Preheat the oven to 350°F and grease the bottom and sides of a 9- by 13-inch baking pan with butter.

In a medium bowl, whisk together the flour, baking powder, and salt, and reserve.

In the bowl of an electric mixer on medium-high speed, beat the butter and granulated sugar until light and fluffy, about 2 minutes. Add the egg and almond extract and beat until combined. Reduce the speed to low, add the flour mixture, and mix until the dough becomes clumpy. Using your hands, pat the dough evenly into the prepared pan, smoothing it as much as possible to a uniform thickness. Bake until the cookie base is just set and the edges begin to brown, about 10 to 12 minutes. Remove from the oven and transfer the baking pan to a wire rack.

In a small bowl, lightly whisk the egg white. Brush the cookie base with the egg white.

TO PREPARE TOPPING: In a medium bowl, combine the apricots, walnuts, almonds, granulated sugar, lemon zest, orange zest, and salt, and stir to combine. Add the butter and use your fingers to mix the ingredients together. Spread the topping mixture evenly over the par-baked cookie base. Lightly press down on the topping mixture to help it

adhere to the cookie base. Return the baking pan to the oven and bake until the nuts are golden brown and fragrant, about 15 to 20 minutes. Remove from the oven and transfer the baking pan to a wire rack.

TO PREPARE GLAZE: In a microwave-safe container, combine the honey, butter, brown sugar, and lemon juice, and heat until bubbly, about 30 seconds. Remove from the microwave, stir to combine, and stir in the orange liqueur. Drizzle the glaze evenly over the topping.

Allow the bar cookies to cool for several hours, then cut into squares in four long rows and six short rows, yielding 24 squares measuring 2 1/4 inches by 2 1/8 inches. The longer they sit, the easier they are to cut, as the toppings and glaze become more secure. The bar cookies become sturdier the next day.

CHAPTER SIX

More
Cookies

Almond Spoons

"All of my recipes are from my childhood," said Sharon Severson of North Oaks. "I have boxes of my mom's old recipes and a file of some of the favorites that I make regularly. This is something she called 'Almond Lace.' She would spool them around the krumkake iron, but I just drape them over a dowel, like a taco shell. They're very pretty on a plate; they're almost like candy." Severson grew up on a farm on the Iron Range, the second-youngest of her Swedish immigrant parents' ten children. "I liked being in the kitchen with my mom," she said. "She was a fantastic cook and baker. We lived off the land. My two daughters laugh when I tell them stories about growing up on the farm. They say I'm like Laura Ingalls in *Little House in the Big Woods.* I'm a city girl now, but you can't take the country out of me."

MAKES 2 DOZEN COOKIES

7 tablespoons unsalted butter
1 scant cup finely chopped almonds
1 cup granulated sugar
1 tablespoon flour
¼ teaspoon vanilla sugar (see Note)
1 tablespoon heavy cream
1 tablespoon half-and-half
1 tablespoon light corn syrup

NOTE Vanilla sugar is available in some supermarkets and specialty food stores. Or make your own by splitting 1 vanilla bean, burying it into ½ pound of granulated sugar, and storing it in a tightly sealed container for 1 week. If you prefer, skip the shaping of the cookie. They also look pretty in their wafer-like appearance straight from the oven. This recipe works well when substituting gluten-free flour for all-purpose flour.

Preheat the oven to 375°F and line the baking sheets with parchment paper.

In a double boiler over gently simmering water (or in a bowl in a microwave oven), melt the butter. Remove from the heat and slightly cool.

In a large bowl, combine the melted butter, almonds, granulated sugar, flour, vanilla sugar, cream, half-and-half, and corn syrup, and mix until thoroughly combined. Shape the dough into 1-inch balls, and place 3 inches apart on the prepared baking sheets, baking 4 to 6 cookies at a time. (The cookies spread greatly.) Bake until lightly golden brown, about 8 minutes. Remove the cookies from the oven.

Carefully slide the parchment paper off the baking sheet onto a flat surface. Using a thin metal spatula, lift the cookies off the parchment paper and, with your hand, gently bend the flat cookie into the shape of a taco shell (the "spoon" of its name). If you prefer, you can drape plastic wrap over a broomstick-size dowel and drape the cookie over it to create the "spoon" shape; cool completely. The shaping takes some practice; the cookies need to be cool enough to hold their shape, but not so cool that they have set and hardened. If the cookies have become too cool, return the parchment paper to the hot baking sheet to warm up the cookies.

Chai Meringues

Creating a chai-seasoned cookie was a natural impulse for Zia McNeal of Maple Grove. "My parents are both from India, and I've always had this preference for what Americans call 'chai spice blend,'" she said. "I looked at a few meringue recipes and added my chai mixture. There are so many rich desserts, and I was looking to offset that with something lighter." While this recipe includes what she calls her "chai magic combination of spices," McNeal also encourages experimentation. "You can make it how you want it to be," she said. "It just has to add up to a teaspoon."

MAKES 6 DOZEN COOKIES

1 cup granulated sugar
1/2 teaspoon ground cardamom
1/4 heaping teaspoon ground cinnamon
1/4 teaspoon ground cloves
3 egg whites, at room temperature
Freshly grated nutmeg, optional

NOTE These cookies are baked in a lower-than-normal temperature oven and are best when prepared on a low-humidity day.

Preheat the oven to 250°F and line the baking sheets with parchment paper.

In a small bowl, whisk together the sugar, cardamom, cinnamon, and cloves, and reserve.

In the bowl of an electric mixer fitted with a whisk attachment on medium-high speed, whip the egg whites until they form soft peaks. Add the sugar-spice mixture, 1 tablespoon at a time, and continue to whip until the meringue forms stiff, glossy (but not dry) peaks.

Carefully spoon the meringue into a piping bag with a large star tip. Pipe cookies into 1 1/2-inch mounds and space about 1 inch apart on the prepared baking sheets (alternatively, you can use 2 teaspoons and drop the meringue on the prepared baking sheets). If you prefer a bit more seasoning, sprinkle the freshly grated nutmeg on the piped meringues (optional). Bake for 90 minutes. Turn off the oven and leave the cookies in the oven for at least 1 hour (do not open the door); this will help dry out the cookies and reduce cracking. Remove the cookies from the oven and transfer them to an airtight container.

Chocolate-Drizzled Churros

The idea of creating a cookie version of the churro, the sweet fried-dough snack, occurred to Lance Swanson of North Branch while he was shopping. "We go to Costco a lot, and I'll buy churros once in a while," he said. "I was eating them and started thinking, 'This would be a good cookie.' I started looking at spritz cookie recipes, and then tweaked the flavors. This is what I came up with." Judges were impressed. "They really capture the churro-ness of churros," said one judge. "This would be a fun State Fair food," said another. Swanson encourages bakers to seek out Mexican chocolate.

MAKES 5 TO 6 DOZEN COOKIES

FOR COOKIES

½ cup plus ⅔ cup granulated sugar, divided

2 ½ teaspoons ground cinnamon, divided

2 ½ cups flour

¼ teaspoon salt

1 cup (2 sticks) unsalted butter, at room temperature

3 egg yolks, at room temperature

1 ½ teaspoons vanilla extract

FOR GANACHE

3.15 ounces Mexican chocolate or semisweet chocolate, chopped (see Note)

1 tablespoon heavy cream or half-and-half

NOTE A recommended chocolate is Abuelita chocolate tablets, which are available at most Mexican supermarkets and specialty stores. Although you can use semisweet chocolate for this recipe, the Mexican chocolate brings the cookie to another level.

TO PREPARE COOKIES: Preheat the oven to 400°F and line the baking sheets with parchment paper.

In a small bowl, combine ½ cup granulated sugar and 1 ½ teaspoons cinnamon, and reserve. In a medium bowl, whisk together the flour, salt, and remaining 1 teaspoon cinnamon, and reserve.

In the bowl of an electric mixer on medium speed, beat the butter until creamy, about 1 minute. Add the remaining ⅔ cup granulated sugar and beat until light and fluffy, about 2 minutes. Add the egg yolks and vanilla extract, and beat until thoroughly combined. Reduce the speed to low, add the flour mixture, and mix until just combined. Transfer the dough to a pastry bag (or cookie press) fitted with a star or ribbon die, and pipe 3-inch long sticks, 1 inch apart, on the prepared baking sheets.

Bake until lightly browned, 9 to 11 minutes. Remove the cookies from the oven and cool for 2 minutes before transferring them to a wire rack until they are cool to the touch. Carefully dredge the cookies in the sugar–cinnamon mixture and return them to a wire rack to cool completely.

TO PREPARE GANACHE: In a double boiler over gently simmering water (or in a bowl in a microwave oven), combine the chocolate and cream (or half-and-half), whisking occasionally until smooth (if using Mexican chocolate, the mixture will be grainy). Transfer the ganache to a pastry bag fitted with a small plain tip (or a plastic sandwich bag with one corner removed with a small cut). Drizzle the ganache over the cookies. Allow the ganache to set before serving.

Chocolate Salami

This easy-to-prepare, no-bake recipe captured the attention of Teresa Haider of St. Paul. "I love to bake," she said. "But it always catches up with me at Christmas. I have intentions to make fancy cookies, but I usually end up making the same old thing." She also appreciates the formula's flexibility. "It would be good with different liqueurs, or different kinds of cookies—amaretti, graham crackers, Biscoff—or dried fruit or coconut," she said. "There are all kinds of combinations that you can try."

MAKES 2 TO 3 DOZEN COOKIES

7 tablespoons salted or unsalted butter

8 to 9 ounces bittersweet chocolate, chopped (see Note)

About 8 to 9 ounces graham crackers, roughly broken into small pieces (about 4 cups broken pieces—see Note)

3 ounces blanched almonds (about 3/4 cup), roughly chopped

2 tablespoons honey

2 tablespoons unsweetened cocoa powder

2 tablespoons rum (see Note)

Powdered sugar, for garnish

NOTE This no-bake dough must be prepared in advance. Along with graham crackers, a variety of options of biscuit/crackers can be used, including amaretti and digestive biscuits. In place of rum, substitute a combination of 1 tablespoon vanilla extract, 1 tablespoon water, a pinch of ground cinnamon, and a pinch of freshly grated nutmeg.

In a double boiler over gently simmering water (or in a bowl in a microwave oven), combine the butter and chocolate, whisking occasionally until smooth. Remove from the heat and cool until the mixture is lukewarm.

In a large bowl, combine the broken graham crackers (or biscuits), almonds, honey, cocoa powder, and rum. Stir in the butter-chocolate mixture until thoroughly combined.

Spoon the mixture onto two large sheets of parchment paper, half the dough on each sheet. Working with your hands, form the dough into rough log shapes, measuring about 8 or 9 inches long. Wrap the dough logs in parchment paper and roll them to even out their shape. Twist the ends of the parchment paper in opposite directions (like a piece of candy). Refrigerate for at least 4 hours.

When ready to serve, remove the dough logs from the refrigerator and bring them to room temperature. Remove the parchment paper. Dust with powdered sugar. Using a thin serrated knife, cut the dough logs into 1/4-inch slices. Store the cookies in an airtight container.

Cranberry Pumpkin-Seed Biscotti

Phyllis Kahn of Minneapolis has a dozen variations in her biscotti repertoire. "This version, with its red and green, is especially for the holidays," she said. Her love affair with biscotti was born, in part, because of the cookie's sturdy practicality. "We have people scattered on both sides of the continent, so we usually end up going somewhere on the holidays," she said. "Transportable things are helpful." Kahn is no stranger to baking competitions, having once received a first-place ribbon at the Minnesota State Fair. "And it was for something I don't even believe in, guiltless cheesecake," she said with a laugh. "I think I put biscotti into an ethnic baking category and got second or third. I'm naturally competitive. I don't enter if I can't win."

MAKES 2 DOZEN BISCOTTI

4 1/2 cups flour

1 teaspoon baking soda

1 teaspoon baking powder

1/2 teaspoon salt

2 teaspoons slightly mashed fennel seeds

2 cups granulated sugar

4 tablespoons (1/2 stick) unsalted butter, melted and cooled

5 eggs, beaten

2 teaspoons vanilla extract

Freshly grated zest from 2 oranges

2 cups dried cranberries

2 cups raw pumpkin seeds (pepitas)

Preheat the oven to 350°F and line the baking sheets with parchment paper.

In a large bowl, whisk together the flour, baking soda, baking powder, salt, and fennel seeds, and reserve.

In the bowl of an electric mixer on medium-high speed, beat the granulated sugar, melted butter, eggs, vanilla extract, and orange zest until thoroughly combined, about 2 minutes. Reduce the speed to low, add the flour mixture, and mix until just combined. Stir in the cranberries and pumpkin seeds.

Divide the dough into 4 equal parts. Form the dough into logs that measure approximately 10 inches long and 2 inches in diameter. Transfer the dough logs to the prepared baking sheets and bake until golden brown and an inserted skewer comes out clean, about 25 to 30 minutes. Remove the dough logs from the oven and cool for 5 minutes. Transfer the dough logs to a cutting board and cut them diagonally into 1/2-inch thick slices.

Reduce the oven temperature to 325°F. Return the slices, cut-side up, to the prepared baking sheets and bake for about 5 minutes. Remove from the oven, turn the biscotti over, and bake an additional 5 minutes. Remove the cookies from the oven and cool for 2 minutes before transferring them to a wire rack to cool completely.

Dark Chocolate Fig Rolls

Elizabeth Davis of Wayzata has always been a Fig Newtons fan. "So I started Googling 'cookies with figs,'" she said. "Up came the Italian *cucidati,* a rolled cookie with a fig-and-nut filling." Davis modified the standard format by adding dark chocolate to the filling, and replacing the recipe's lemon icing with a mocha ganache. "I always like to do new things," she said. "I tend to not repeat myself. If you saw my house, there are recipes everywhere." Cookbooks, too. "I have a gazillion cookbooks," she said. "When I go to a bookstore, I go right to the cooking section. I couldn't care less about the other books."

MAKES 2 DOZEN COOKIES

FOR COOKIES

½ cup (1 stick) unsalted butter, at room temperature
¼ cup granulated sugar
¼ cup packed light brown sugar
¼ teaspoon baking soda
1 egg
1 teaspoon vanilla extract
½ teaspoon salt
1 ¾ cups flour, plus extra for rolling dough

FOR FIG FILLING

1 cup diced dried figs
½ cup finely chopped pitted dates
½ cup freshly squeezed orange juice
⅓ cup diced candied orange peel (or freshly grated zest from 1 orange; see Note)
2 tablespoons granulated sugar
¼ teaspoon ground cinnamon
⅓ cup finely chopped walnuts
1 cup dark chocolate chips

FOR MOCHA GANACHE

1 cup dark chocolate chips, divided
½ cup heavy cream
1 teaspoon instant espresso powder

NOTE This dough must be prepared in advance. Candied orange peel is available in the baking aisle of most supermarkets. Substitute freshly grated orange zest for the candied orange peel. Or to make your own candied orange peel, see page 142.

TO PREPARE COOKIES: In the bowl of an electric mixer on medium-high speed, beat the butter for 1 minute. Add the granulated sugar, brown sugar, and baking soda, and beat until light and fluffy, about 2 minutes. Add the egg, vanilla extract, and salt, and mix until thoroughly combined. Reduce the speed to low, add the flour, and mix until just combined. Divide the dough into two equal pieces. Form the dough into rectangles, wrap in plastic wrap, and refrigerate for at least 3 hours.

TO PREPARE FIG FILLING: In a small saucepan over medium-high heat, combine the figs, dates, orange juice, candied orange peel (or freshly grated orange zest), granulated sugar, and cinnamon. Bring to a boil, then reduce the heat to medium-low and simmer until the mixture is soft and thick, about 5 to 8 minutes. Remove from the heat and stir in the walnuts. Set the mixture aside to cool to room temperature. Once cooled, stir in the chocolate chips.

TO ASSEMBLE COOKIES: Preheat the oven to 375°F and line the baking sheets with parchment paper.

Remove the dough from the refrigerator and allow it to rest at room temperature for 10 minutes.

On a lightly floured surface using a lightly floured rolling pin, roll one of the pieces of dough into a 8- by 10-inch rectangle.

Cut the rectangle into two 4- by 10-inch strips. Portion ¼ of the fig filling down the center of each strip. Lift one long side of the dough up and over the filling, and repeat with the opposite side to enclose the filling (fold the dough as if folding a business-size letter). Pinch the 2 sides together at the edges. Carefully transfer the roll to the prepared baking sheet, placing it seam-side down. Repeat with the second strip of the dough, then repeat the entire process with the second rectangle.

Bake until lightly browned, about 12 minutes. Remove the rolls from the oven, cool for 2 minutes, then slice each roll into 1-inch cookies, cutting diagonally. Transfer the cookies to a wire rack to cool completely.

TO PREPARE MOCHA GANACHE: Place ¾ cup chocolate chips in a medium bowl. Place a wire rack over wax paper or parchment paper.

In a small saucepan over medium heat, bring the cream to a boil and stir in the espresso powder. Pour the cream mixture over the chocolate chips and stir until smooth, adding more chips, if necessary (up to the remaining ¼ cup chocolate chips), to reach the desired consistency. Allow the ganache to cool until it has thickened but remains liquid. Drizzle the ganache over the cookies. Allow the ganache to set before serving.

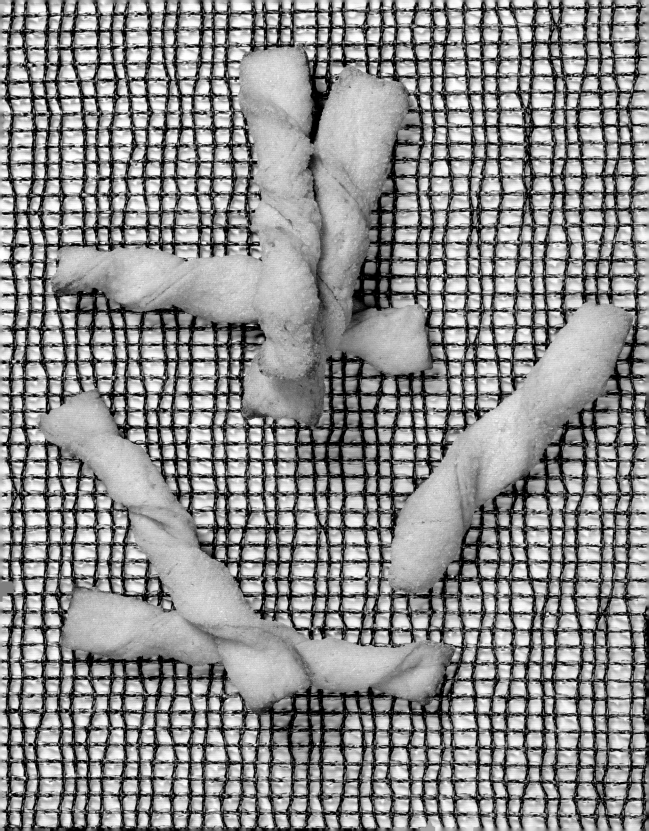

German Sour Cream Twists

Rosemary Hall of St. Louis Park picked up this recipe decades ago from her college roommate. It's a family favorite that stretched back several generations. "They're flaky, almost like pastry," she said. "They're a beautiful addition to a cookie plate." Her voracious reading habit led her to entering the contest. "I read cookbooks the way other people read novels," she said. "I knew that this recipe was different because I've read so many cookbooks, and I've never seen a recipe exactly like this one."

MAKES 5 DOZEN COOKIES

3 ½ cups flour

1 teaspoon salt

½ cup shortening, chilled and cut into small pieces

½ cup (1 stick) unsalted butter, chilled and cut into small pieces

1 envelope (¼ ounce) active dry yeast

¾ cup sour cream

1 extra-large egg plus 2 extra-large egg yolks, well beaten (see Note)

1 teaspoon vanilla extract

1 cup granulated sugar, divided

NOTE This dough must be prepared in advance. The extra-large egg yolks make the dough easier to work with. Use flavored sugars, such as vanilla, cinnamon, or cardamom, or add toasted finely ground nuts with the sugar. Adding chocolate is another possibility.

In a large bowl, whisk together the flour and salt. Using a pastry blender, cut in the shortening and butter until the mixture resembles coarse meal. In a small bowl, combine the yeast with 2 tablespoons of warm water and stir to dissolve. Add the yeast mixture, sour cream, beaten eggs and egg yolks, and vanilla extract to the flour mixture, stirring until thoroughly combined. Cover the bowl with a damp cloth and refrigerate for 2 hours.

When ready to bake, preheat the oven to 375°F and line the baking sheets with parchment paper.

Remove the bowl from the refrigerator and divide the dough in half, keeping the second portion refrigerated while preparing the first. Divide the granulated sugar in half.

On a lightly sugared surface using a rolling pin, roll the dough to an 8- by 16-inch rectangle. Working quickly, fold one end in and fold the other end to cover, as if folding a business-size letter. Sprinkle the dough with granulated sugar. Flip the dough over and roll to the same 8- by 16-inch size. Fold again, sprinkle again, roll again. Repeat the process a third time.

Sprinkle more granulated sugar over the rolled dough. Cut into 1- by 4-inch strips. Twist each strip, stretching the dough slightly. Repeat the process with the second half of the dough and the remaining granulated sugar.

Place the twisted strips 2 inches apart on the prepared baking sheets. Bake until lightly brown, about 10 to 12 minutes. Remove the cookies from the oven and cool for 2 minutes before transferring them to a wire rack to cool completely.

Gingerbread Cornmeal Biscotti

For this softer take on biscotti, Cynthia Baxter of Minneapolis based her recipe on her affectionate recollection of the biscotti at the former Lucia's Restaurant in Minneapolis. That version incorporated finely ground yellow cornmeal, an addition that Baxter believes dials back biscotti's trademark hard-as-nails texture. Gingerbread accents also set this biscotti apart. "Sometimes gingerbreads can be so spicy, but I didn't want that, I wanted warm flavors," said Baxter. "I looked at a ton of gingerbread recipes and then I started playing around with ingredients."

MAKES 4 DOZEN COOKIES

FOR CRANBERRIES

1 cup dried cranberries

1/2 to 3/4 cup apple brandy (see Note)

FOR COOKIES

1 1/2 cups flour, plus extra for shaping dough

1/2 cup finely ground yellow cornmeal

1/2 teaspoon baking powder

1/2 teaspoon baking soda

1/2 teaspoon salt

1 1/2 teaspoons ground cinnamon

1/2 teaspoons ground ginger

1/4 teaspoon ground cloves

1/8 teaspoon freshly ground black pepper

2 eggs

2 tablespoons molasses

1 teaspoon vanilla extract

1/2 cup (1 stick) unsalted butter, at room temperature

1/2 cup granulated sugar

1/2 cup packed light brown sugar

1/2 cup shelled and chopped pistachios (see Note)

1 egg white

FOR GLAZE

8 ounces white chocolate

1 teaspoon canola oil or other flavor-neutral oil

Chopped pistachios for garnish, optional

NOTE Portions of this recipe must be prepared in advance. Baker Cynthia Baxter prefers Calvados as her apple brandy of choice. Or, skip the apple brandy and cover the cranberries in boiling water (or boiling apple cider) for 5 minutes, then drain before chopping and adding to the dough. Baxter also prefers using lightly salted pistachios.

TO PREPARE CRANBERRIES: Place the cranberries in a small bowl and cover with the apple brandy, and let sit for at least 2 hours or overnight. Drain before adding the cranberries to the dough.

TO PREPARE COOKIES: Chop the cranberries, and reserve. In a medium bowl, whisk together the flour, cornmeal, baking powder, baking soda, salt, cinnamon, ginger, cloves, and black pepper, and reserve.

In a medium bowl, whisk together the eggs, molasses, and vanilla extract, and reserve.

In the bowl of an electric mixer on medium-high speed, beat the butter until creamy, about 1 minute. Add the granulated sugar and brown sugar and beat until light and fluffy, about 2 minutes. Reduce the speed to medium, add the egg mixture, and beat until thoroughly combined; the mixture will look curdled. Reduce the speed to low, add the flour mixture, and mix until just combined. Stir in the cranberries and pistachios. Cover the bowl with plastic wrap and refrigerate for 1 hour.

When ready to bake, preheat the oven to 350°F and line the baking sheets with parchment paper.

On a lightly floured surface (with lightly floured hands), pat the dough into an 8- by 8-inch square. Cut the square into 3 equal rectangles, then shape the rectangles so they are 1 inch thick and 10 inches long. Place the rectangles on the prepared baking sheets, leaving as much room as possible between them, as they will spread while baking.

In a small bowl, whisk together the egg white and 1 teaspoon water until foamy. Brush the tops of the rectangles with the egg wash. Bake for 25 minutes. Remove from the oven and cool until the rectangles are easy to handle, about 15 minutes. Transfer the rectangles to a wire rack and cool for an additional 5 to 10 minutes.

Transfer the rectangles to a cutting board and, using a serrated knife, slice them crossways into ½-inch slices. Place the slices back on the prepared baking sheets (they can be placed close together, but not touching) and bake for an additional 12 to 15 minutes. Remove from the oven and cool the biscotti for at least 30 minutes.

TO PREPARE GLAZE: In a double boiler over gently simmering water (or in a bowl in a microwave oven), melt the white chocolate, whisking occasionally until smooth. Add the canola oil and whisk to combine. Arrange the biscotti, flat side down, on wax paper or parchment paper. Drizzle the glaze over the biscotti (or dip the biscotti in the glaze) and garnish with the pistachios (optional). Allow the glaze to set before serving.

Macadamia Nut Tarts

Trish Cowle of Mendota Heights adapted this recipe from one in a long-forgotten cookbook. Along with graham cracker chocolate rollouts, sugar cookies, and bars, Cowle's holiday baking schedule always includes Macadamia Nut Tarts. "They get rave reviews. I have family members who insist on them," she said. When Cowle first encountered the recipe, the main ingredient captured her attention. "I love macadamias and I thought, 'This has to be great,'" she said. "But then again, I love nuts."

MAKES 4 DOZEN COOKIES (MINI-MUFFIN SIZE)

FOR CRUST

3 cups flour, plus extra for rolling dough

1/2 cup cornstarch

1/2 teaspoon salt

1 1/2 cups (3 sticks) unsalted butter, at room temperature, plus extra for tart pans or mini-muffin pans

2/3 cup granulated sugar

Dried lemon zest from 1 large lemon (see Note)

FOR TOPPING

10 tablespoons (1 stick plus 2 tablespoons) unsalted butter

1/2 cup packed light brown sugar

1/3 cup granulated sugar

2 1/2 tablespoons heavy cream

3 cups macadamia nuts, coarsely chopped

NOTE This dough must be prepared in advance. To prepare dried lemon zest, spread the freshly grated zest from 1 large lemon on wax paper and allow to air-dry overnight. Try other nuts instead of macadamia, if you prefer.

TO PREPARE CRUST: Preheat the oven to 350°F and grease the mini-tart or mini-muffin pans.

In a medium bowl, whisk together the flour, cornstarch, and salt, and reserve.

In the bowl of an electric mixer on medium-high speed, beat the butter until creamy, about 1 minute. Add the granulated sugar and lemon zest, and beat until light and fluffy, about 2 minutes. Reduce the speed to low, add the flour mixture, and mix just until the dough is crumbly.

On a lightly floured surface using a lightly floured rolling pin, roll the dough to 3/8-inch thickness. Using a 2- or 3-inch biscuit cutter (depending on the size of mini-tart pan or mini-muffin pan), cut the dough and transfer the dough rounds to the prepared pans, pressing the dough into the pan and leaving a well in the center of each cookie (or form the dough into balls, press the dough balls into the pans, and form the desired shape). Prick the dough with a fork and bake until light brown, about 16 to 18 minutes. Remove the pans from the oven and cool for 10 minutes. Then remove the cookies from the pans and place them on a wire rack to cool completely.

TO PREPARE TOPPING: In a medium saucepan over medium heat, combine the butter, brown sugar, and granulated sugar. Stir constantly over medium heat until the mixture comes to a boil. Boil without stirring, until the mixture thickens and large bubbles begin to form, about 1 minute. Remove the pan from the heat; stir in the cream and nuts. Spoon 1 to 2 tablespoons (depending on pan size) topping into each tart crust and cool completely.

Nutmeg Sticks

To the best of her recollection, Kathie Nelson's signature Christmas cookie dates to the late 1960s, when a friend raved about a recipe she'd picked up from a utility company promotion. For Nelson, the details sounded just right. "My family loves the nutmeg and buttery rum flavors," she said. The Richfield resident gave the cookie a shot but found that rolling and cutting dough was an activity too time-consuming for her baking habits. So she improvised and reached for her cookie press. The impulse was a good one, and she's been making these eye-catching, spritz-inspired treats ever since.

MAKES 8 DOZEN COOKIES

FOR COOKIES

3 cups flour

1 teaspoon freshly grated nutmeg

¼ teaspoon salt

1 cup (2 sticks) unsalted butter, at room temperature

¾ cup granulated sugar

1 egg

2 teaspoons vanilla extract

2 teaspoons rum extract (or 1 to 2 tablespoons rum, to taste)

FOR FROSTING

⅓ cup (5 ⅓ tablespoons) unsalted butter, at room temperature

2 cups powdered sugar

2 teaspoons vanilla extract

2 teaspoons rum extract (or 1 to 2 tablespoons rum, to taste)

2 tablespoons heavy cream

Freshly grated nutmeg for garnish

TO PREPARE COOKIES: Preheat the oven to 350°F and line the baking sheets with parchment paper.

In a medium bowl, whisk together the flour, nutmeg, and salt, and reserve.

In the bowl of an electric mixer on medium-high speed, beat the butter until creamy, about 1 minute. Gradually add the granulated sugar and beat until light and fluffy, about

2 minutes. Add the egg and beat until thoroughly combined. Add the vanilla extract and rum extract, and beat until thoroughly combined. Reduce the speed to low, add the flour mixture, and mix until just combined.

Spoon the dough into a cookie press fitted with a small (⅝-inch) star plate. Holding the press in an almost horizontal position, form long rolls on the prepared baking sheets (rolls can be placed close together, as these cookies do not spread when baked). Cut the rolls into 3-inch sticks. Bake 10 minutes. Remove the cookies from the oven and allow them to cool completely on the baking sheets before transferring them to a wire rack.

TO PREPARE FROSTING: In the bowl of an electric mixer on medium speed, beat the butter until creamy, about 1 minute. Gradually add the powdered sugar and beat until light and fluffy, about 2 minutes. Add the vanilla extract and rum extract, and beat until well combined. Add the cream and beat until the frosting is light and creamy. Frost each cookie and sprinkle with nutmeg.

Raspberry Truffle Tartlets

Tricia Hall, a busy family physician in Minneapolis, turns to baking as her self-care. "It's my therapy after a long day at work," she said. "I get home and I like to do something with my hands instead of my head. I'll often bake late at night and decompress that way." Chocolate and raspberry are two favorite tastes, so Hall used them as a starting point. A real "aha!" moment came when she added raspberry liqueur. Her nursing staff proved to be valuable taste-testers, and her mother-in-law added the final touch, a festive white chocolate drizzle. Her advice: savor them slowly. "They're not like a chocolate chip cookie," she said. "They're more like a truffle. You can get overloaded on the sugar high."

MAKES 4 DOZEN COOKIES

Nonstick cooking spray
2 1/2 cups flour
2/3 cup unsweetened cocoa powder
1 teaspoon baking soda
1/4 teaspoon salt
1 cup (2 sticks) plus 2 tablespoons unsalted butter, at room temperature
3/4 cup packed light brown sugar
2/3 cup granulated sugar
2 eggs
1 teaspoon vanilla extract
2 1/2 tablespoons raspberry liqueur
1 1/2 cups semisweet chocolate chips
8 ounces raspberry preserves
2/3 cup white chocolate chips

Preheat the oven to 350°F. Lightly coat mini-muffin tins with cooking spray. Place a wire rack over wax paper or parchment paper.

In a medium bowl, whisk together the flour, cocoa powder, baking soda, and salt, and reserve.

In the bowl of an electric mixer on medium-high speed, beat the butter until creamy, about 1 minute. Add the brown sugar and granulated sugar, and beat until light and fluffy, about 2 minutes. Add the eggs, one at a time, beating well after each addition. Add the vanilla extract and raspberry liqueur, and

beat until thoroughly combined. Reduce the speed to low, add the flour mixture, and mix until just combined. Stir in the semisweet chocolate chips.

Shape the dough into 1-inch balls. Place the balls into the prepared mini-muffin tins and bake 7 minutes. Remove the tins from the oven and, using the back of a spoon, immediately (and gently) flatten the tops of the tartlets. Transfer the tins to the prepared wire rack and cool for about 10 minutes. Using a small knife, carefully separate the tartlets from the tins and transfer them to the prepared wire rack to cool completely.

In a small bowl, stir the preserves. Place 1/2 teaspoon preserves on top of each tartlet and carefully spread.

In a double boiler over gently simmering water (or in a bowl in a microwave oven), melt the white chocolate chips, whisking occasionally until smooth. Drizzle the melted white chocolate over the tartlets. Allow the white chocolate to set before serving.

Royal Sweets with Chocolate Balsamic Sauce

A self-described "Nordic food geek and meatball historian," Patrice Johnson of Roseville stumbled on her winning formula in an "elderly but beloved" book from Time-Life's popular 1960s *Foods of the World* series. The recipe sparked a happy childhood memory. "My mom always made these meringue cookies for Christmas," she said. "I loved them." Enriching meringue with cocoa powder came from a chocolate baking contest that Johnson entered, and the vinegar-infused chocolate filling was suggested by a student in one of her cooking classes. "Easily the most beautiful cookie on the table," raved one judge, while others declared "Wow" and "Gorgeous."

MAKES 2 DOZEN COOKIES

FOR COOKIES

4 egg whites, at room temperature

⅛ teaspoon cream of tartar

Pinch of salt

1 cup superfine sugar

2 tablespoons unsweetened cocoa powder, sifted or whisked to remove lumps

FOR SAUCE

3 ounces dark chocolate

⅓ cup heavy cream

¼ cup packed light brown sugar

1 tablespoon balsamic vinegar

2 tablespoons unsalted butter, cold

1 teaspoon vanilla extract

NOTE These cookies bake in a lower-than-normal-temperature oven.

TO PREPARE COOKIES: Preheat the oven to 250°F and line the baking sheets with parchment paper.

In the bowl of an electric mixer fitted with a whisk attachment on medium-high speed, whip the egg whites, cream of tartar, and salt until they form soft peaks. Slowly add the superfine sugar and continue to whip until the meringue forms stiff, glossy (but not dry) peaks. Using a rubber spatula, carefully fold in the cocoa powder.

Using a pastry bag fitted with a star tip (or a plastic bag, with a corner cut out), fill the bag with batter and pipe a basket-shaped circular cookie, 1½ inches wide and 1½ inches tall, with a small indented opening in the center (or make a tiny depression in the top of the cookie with a wet finger or the back of a wet spoon). Alternately, use a small scoop to drop mounds of batter on the prepared baking sheets and then make the indentation on top. Repeat with the remaining batter. Bake until the cookies are dry and crisp on the outside but tender on the inside, 50 to 60 minutes. If the cookies start to take on any color, reduce the heat to 200°F. Remove the cookies from the oven and cool 5 minutes before transferring them to a wire rack to cool completely.

TO PREPARE SAUCE: In a small saucepan over low heat, combine the chocolate, cream, and brown sugar, stirring occasionally until the chocolate has melted. Stir in the vinegar. Remove the pan from the heat and stir in the butter until melted. Stir in the vanilla extract and cool slightly. Spoon the sauce into the center of the cookies.

Tiramisu Twists

While hosting an Italian-themed dinner party, Joanne Holtmeier of Edina engaged in a favorite culinary exercise: transforming beloved standards—in this case, tiramisu—into cookies. "Cookies are easy, casual, and fun to serve," she said. Her starting point was an eggnog-inspired cookie from a recipe of her husband's grandmother as a stand-in for tiramisu's traditional ladyfingers. Our suggestion: instead of rum extract, consider spiced rum. One option is Ålander, the Nordic-style spiced rum from Far North Spirits, produced in Hallock, Minnesota.

MAKES 2 TO 3 DOZEN COOKIES

FOR COOKIES

2 1/2 cups flour plus extra for rolling dough
1/4 teaspoon baking powder
1/4 teaspoon salt
1 cup (2 sticks) unsalted butter, at room temperature
3/4 cup granulated sugar
2 eggs
1 teaspoon vanilla extract
1 1/4 teaspoons rum extract
1 1/2 teaspoons instant espresso powder
2 tablespoons unsweetened cocoa powder

FOR MASCARPONE GLAZE

1 1/2 cups powdered sugar, plus more as needed
1/4 cup mascarpone cheese, at room temperature
1 1/2 teaspoons heavy cream (or milk), plus more as needed
1 to 2 tablespoons brewed espresso (or coffee), at room temperature
Finely chopped dark chocolate, for garnish

NOTE This dough must be prepared in advance.

TO PREPARE COOKIES: In a medium bowl, whisk together the flour, baking powder, and salt, and reserve.

In the bowl of an electric mixer on medium-high speed, beat the butter until creamy, about 1 minute. Add the granulated sugar and beat until light and fluffy, about 2 minutes. Add 1 egg, 1 egg yolk (reserving egg white), and vanilla extract, and beat until thoroughly combined. Reduce the speed to low, add the flour mixture, and mix until just combined.

Form the dough into 3 equal portions and transfer each portion to a separate medium bowl. Mix the rum extract into the first dough, mix the espresso powder into the second dough, and mix the cocoa powder into the third dough.

Divide each type of dough into 2 equal pieces. Form the dough into rectangles, wrap in plastic wrap, and refrigerate for 1 hour.

On a lightly floured surface, roll each portion of the dough into ropes about 16 inches long. Lay a rope of the rum-flavored dough next to a rope of the espresso-flavored dough next to a rope of the cocoa-flavored dough (espresso-flavored dough should be in the middle), brushing each layer with the reserved egg white to help the layers adhere to one another. Press down lightly to slightly flatten and adhere the layers together. Repeat with the remaining ropes of dough. Refrigerate the dough for about 10 minutes.

When ready to bake, preheat the oven to 350°F and line the baking sheets with parchment paper.

Using a sharp knife, cut the dough into 1-inch-wide pieces. Take each piece and press it together to secure, then roll it between your hands or on a very lightly floured surface to make a 3-inch baton. Repeat with the remaining dough, and place 2 inches apart on the prepared baking sheets. Bake until the tops of the cookies are set and slightly cracked, about 8 to 10 minutes. Remove the cookies from the oven and cool for 5 minutes before transferring them to a wire rack to cool completely.

TO PREPARE MASCARPONE GLAZE: Place a wire rack over wax paper or parchment paper. In the bowl of an electric mixer on low speed, combine the powdered sugar, mascarpone, cream (or milk), and espresso (or coffee), and mix until combined. Increase the speed to medium and mix until the glaze is smooth and creamy, adjusting with powdered sugar or cream (or milk) to achieve the desired consistency. Transfer the glaze to a plastic bag, cut out the corner, and pipe decorative stripes or swirls of the glaze on the top of each cookie. Immediately top with the finely chopped chocolate and place the cookies on the prepared wire rack. Allow the glaze to set before serving.

CONTENTS

CHAPTER SEVEN

Cookie Memories

Ambassadors of Scandinavian Treats

LEE SVITAK DEAN

RICK AND I were in the throes of planning a national conference for the Association of Food Journalists as we arranged for one quintessential Minnesota experience after another, in an effort to capture the attention— and delight—of the food writers who would descend on Minneapolis. There would be a progressive dinner (a Midwestern tradition) as the crowd walked to three top-shelf restaurants for different courses. We would talk flour mills and wild rice, visit the General Mills test kitchen, and—with great anticipation by the participants—head to the State Fair (sculpted butterheads of dairy princesses! Reuben-on-a-stick! deep-fried candy bars!).

"What else reflects Minnesota?" I asked my mother, as I was briefing her on the plans.

"Well, we could make Norwegian treats for a coffee break," she suggested, referring to her sister and herself.

That got my attention. I had been going to these food conferences for more than a decade, and none had offered such a homespun moment. While her sister focused on lefse, the Scandinavian potato flatbread, my mother broke out the sandbakkel tins, the small fluted molds that had been in our family for decades. Under the skilled hands of my grandmother, and later my mother, and with the help of any willing assistant, these tins had shaped hundreds, if not thousands, of the specialty sugar cookies, whose name means "sand pastry" in Norwegian.

When we wheeled the cart with treats into the conference ballroom, the attendees made a beeline for the plentiful table. "How did you make these?" the reporters asked while nibbling on the snacks as they interviewed the smiling bakers.

Make no mistake, sandbakkels take more effort than a drop or refrigerator cookie, but not by much. A small amount of dough is pressed into the sides and bottom of a cookie tin until the interior is uniformly covered. The effort isn't difficult, but like any kitchen technique, it takes practice to master.

I learned how to make sandbakkels as a grade-schooler at the red metal table in my grandmother's kitchen. "Not too much dough, and keep it even throughout," she reminded me while smoothing out the blob on the bottom and filling in the thin spots on the sides. By the time I was in high school, I was a pro at shaping the cookies and ready to trash talk anyone with a less-than-perfect result.

"Looking a little lumpy there," I'd tease anyone with a misshapen cookie.

We rarely broke out the recipe for anything beyond the Christmas holidays, but one of those occasions included an eighth-grade history project where we had to bring in something that reflected our family. With the help of my grandmother and mother, we made enough sandbakkels for the whole class, which assured a grade of "A" for me and a lot of happy students.

Many years and sandbakkels later, in 2020 when the pandemic hit, I didn't see my mother for most of a year. Then in her late 80s, she lived across the country from me but, as December loomed, I decided it was time to take the risk—pre-vaccine, but with a face mask—to see her.

Not long after we embraced, we reached for the sandbakkel tins and mixed up the

Laverne Svitak presses cookie dough into a sandbakkel tin.

simple dough: butter, sugar, flour, eggs, and almond extract. Without hesitation, she scooped a perfectly sized bit of dough and set to work, her fingers pressing the mixture into the crinkles of the tin without pause or frustration, with the dexterity of someone who had mastered this skill long ago.

We worked in silence, shoulder to shoulder, tin to tin, the Christmas lights glowing, the winter sun low in the sky, a cookie linking us to family who lived in Norway more than a century ago.

That's what a cookie can do.

Sandbakkels

MAKES 3 DOZEN COOKIES FROM A 3-INCH DIAMETER ROUND SANDBAKKEL TIN

1 cup (2 sticks) butter, at room temperature
1 cup granulated sugar
2 eggs
$1/2$ teaspoon almond extract
2 $3/4$ cups flour, plus extra for rolling dough

NOTE The tins vary in size and shape and the amount of dough needed for each will be dependent on the tin. While the cookies are often served simply as is, they can be sprinkled with powdered sugar or be used as a tart shell for fillings, such as custard or fruit. Not that my grandmother or mother would do that. "Why would you gild the lily?" was the response to the occasional question.

Preheat the oven to 350°F.

In the bowl of an electric mixer on medium-high speed, beat the butter until creamy, about 1 minute. Add the granulated sugar and beat until light and fluffy, about 2 minutes. Add the eggs and almond extract, and beat until thoroughly combined. Reduce the speed to low. Add the flour in three additions, mixing until the dough is smooth. Cover the bowl with plastic wrap and refrigerate for 30 minutes.

For a 3-inch sandbakkel tin, take about 1 tablespoon of dough (see Note), roll into a ball and press the dough evenly into the sides and bottom of the tin, beginning with the bottom and working up. The dough should be about $1/8$ inch thick in the tin. Repeat with the remaining dough and tins. Place the tins on a rimmed baking sheet. Bake until lightly browned, about 13 to 15 minutes.

Remove the sandbakkel tins from the oven and transfer them to a wire rack to cool until they can be handled easily, about 2 minutes. Then invert the tin and gently pinch the sides of it until the cookie drops out onto the wire rack to cool completely. If it's difficult to remove the cookie from the tin, put it back in the oven to warm up a bit and try again.

Laverne's Million-Dollar Cookies

It's not a new phenomenon to reference a "million dollar" recipe. They've been appearing since at least the 1950s, though it's tough to find out why those older recipes took the name. While there are similar recipes out there to this one from the Svitak repertoire, coconut offers the signature—and different—ingredient to the mix for a terrific combo. If a Russian tea cake merged with a coconut cookie, this would be the result.

MAKES 2 1/2 DOZEN COOKIES

2 cups flour

1/2 teaspoon salt

1/2 teaspoon baking soda

3/4 cup finely chopped walnuts or pecans

1/2 cup sweetened shredded coconut

1 cup (2 sticks) butter, at room temperature, plus extra for pressing dough

1/2 cup granulated sugar, plus extra for pressing dough

1/2 cup packed light brown sugar

1 egg

1 teaspoon vanilla extract

Preheat the oven to 350°F and line the baking sheets with parchment paper.

In a medium bowl, stir together the flour, salt, baking soda, walnuts (or pecans), and coconut, and reserve.

In the bowl of an electric mixer on medium-high speed, beat the butter, granulated sugar, and brown sugar until light and fluffy, about 2 minutes. Add the egg and vanilla extract, and beat until thoroughly combined.

Reduce the speed to low. Add the flour mixture in three additions, mixing until just combined.

Shape the dough into 1-inch balls, and place 2 inches apart on the prepared baking sheets. Place about 1 cup granulated sugar into a shallow bowl. With the flat bottom of a glass, carefully press it onto a cookie, flattening it until the dough is about 1/4-inch thick. Dip the glass bottom into granulated sugar and repeat with the remaining cookies. Bake until the cookies are set and lightly browned, about 10 to 12 minutes. Remove the cookies from the oven and cool for 2 minutes before transferring them to a wire rack to cool completely.

Salted Peanut Cookies

As so often happens with family recipes, Lee thought these occasional treats in the Svitak cookie jar were her mother's invention. She found out much later that her mother's recipe was actually from Betty Crocker in the 1963 *Cooky Book*, which noted that it was the most popular "cooky" of 1950–55. Of course, Lee had to tinker with the recipe to update it, because that is what bakers do. The cookie reminds her of a very fresh Pearson's Salted Nut Roll, the irresistible candy bar made by the St. Paul company of the same name, where her father worked for decades. A 25-pound candy bar was occasionally handmade for special events—and this cookie brings back those taste memories. Don Svitak would have eaten these with delight.

MAKES 5 DOZEN COOKIES

3/4 cup flour
1/2 teaspoon baking soda
1/2 teaspoon baking powder
1 1/2 cups rolled oats
1/2 cup butter (1 stick), at room temperature
3/4 cup packed light brown sugar
1/4 cup granulated sugar
1 egg
1 teaspoon vanilla extract
1 cup salted peanuts, roughly chopped

Preheat the oven to 350°F and line the baking sheets with parchment paper.

In a medium bowl, whisk together the flour, baking soda, baking powder, and rolled oats, and reserve.

In the bowl of an electric mixer on medium-high speed, beat the butter, brown sugar, and granulated sugar until light and fluffy, about 2 minutes. Add the egg and vanilla extract, and beat until thoroughly combined. Reduce the speed to low. Add the flour mixture in three additions, mixing until just combined. Stir in the salted peanuts.

Shape the dough into 1-inch balls, and place 2 inches apart on the prepared baking sheets. Bake until the cookies are set and lightly browned, about 8 to 10 minutes. Remove the cookies from the oven and cool for 2 minutes before transferring them to a wire rack to cool completely.

Cinnamon Dreams

Experiments in the kitchen (occasionally known as "mistakes") can end up with great results, at least on a good day. Such was the case as Lee attempted to make her mother's applesauce cookie recipe. But Lee was preoccupied and, though she had laid out all the ingredients, didn't remember until her cookies were in the oven that she had forgotten to add the applesauce to the dough. She let the cookies cool slightly before taking a nibble. To her surprise, they tasted great and she baked the remainder, adding these new cinnamon cookies to her list of favorites.

MAKES 4 DOZEN COOKIES

2 ¼ cups flour
½ teaspoon baking soda
½ teaspoon baking powder
½ teaspoon salt
¾ teaspoon plus 2 teaspoons ground cinnamon, divided
¼ teaspoon ground cloves
½ cup granulated sugar
6 tablespoons (¾ stick) butter, at room temperature
1 cup packed light brown sugar
1 egg

Preheat the oven to 350°F and line the baking sheets with parchment paper.

In a medium bowl, whisk together flour, baking soda, baking powder, salt, ¾ teaspoon cinnamon, and cloves, and reserve.

In a shallow bowl, stir together ½ cup granulated sugar and remaining 2 teaspoons cinnamon, and reserve.

In the bowl of an electric mixer on medium-high speed, beat the butter and brown sugar until light and fluffy, about 2 minutes. Add the egg and beat until thoroughly combined. Reduce the speed to low. Add the flour mixture in three additions, mixing until just combined.

Shape the dough into 1-inch balls (the dough is a bit crumbly). Roll the balls in the reserved cinnamon sugar before placing them 2 inches apart on the prepared baking sheets. Bake until lightly browned, 9 to 10 minutes. Remove the cookies from the oven and cool for 2 minutes before rolling them again in the remaining cinnamon sugar. Place the cookies on a wire rack to cool completely.

A Cookie by Many Names

LEE SVITAK DEAN

WHEN I THINK OF RUSSIAN TEA CAKES, I remember the week of making seven hundred cookies. Yes, I was crazed, even by my own standards. Big events do that to me.

The occasion was my daughter's senior art show at her college in Iowa. It was December and she needed a holiday-themed spread of goodies to serve during the opening reception for the hungry crowd of students, faculty, friends, and family who would descend on her exhibit.

A week before the gathering, after the dinner dishes were finished, I reached for the worn *Betty Crocker's Cooky Book* (yes, that's the way Betty spelled it) and baked for seven nights in a row, one hundred cookies at a time. At the end of that baking frenzy, I packed up the tins and Tupperware to be transported through snowy cornfields along the two-lane highway to Luther College.

I baked other cookies for the reception, of course. Even I wouldn't make seven hundred Russian tea cakes. But those I remember, probably because they are a favorite of mine. The little mounds of powdered sugar that look like snowballs have been on every family holiday cookie plate for as long as I can remember, whether it was at the house of my grandmother or mother.

December was the only time I saw the cookies, which may be part of their appeal. Those treats are wrapped in fond memories of the hustle and bustle, warm hugs, and crisp air that surrounded us as one relative after another opened the front door, stomped off the snow, and settled into our merrymaking.

It was not only the cookies' holiday appearance that prompts me to grab one mound, then another. The draw for me is that the tea cakes aren't very sweet. The dominant flavors are butter and ground nuts . . . and powdered sugar. Lots of powdered sugar. These may be the only cookies that need a warning: do not inhale while eating (that powdered sugar dust can be dangerous!)—and definitely don't eat while wearing black.

Then there is the name, which enchants me. Or the many names for the cookie: Russian tea cakes, Mexican wedding cakes, pecan sandies, pecan butter balls, and butter balls.

The first Mexican wedding cake recipe doesn't turn up in cookbooks until the 1950s, though its heritage clearly extends back generations, if not centuries, perhaps in part because the cookies are so durable—they travel well and can be kept for a long time. At my grandmother's house, they were packed in tins weeks before the holidays arrived and stored on the cold stairs that led to the attic.

The cookies probably date back to medieval Arab cuisine, where even then they were saved for special occasions and made of what would have been expensive ingredients at the time—butter, sugar, and nuts. The treats were brought by the Moors to Spain, where they are called *polvorones* (based on the Spanish word for dust, *polvo*). Like any good food, they spread across Europe and eventually crossed the ocean, where they traveled across the New World and to Mexico and beyond.

Whether made of pecans, almonds, or hazelnuts—or cashews in the Philippines, macadamias in Hawaii—the nutty treats belong at the world table. And at my table, as well. But this year I'll stick to a single batch.

Russian Tea Cakes

MAKES 4 DOZEN COOKIES

2 ¼ cups flour

¼ teaspoon salt

1 cup (2 sticks) unsalted butter, at room temperature

½ cup powdered sugar, plus more for rolling

1 teaspoon vanilla extract

¾ cup finely chopped nuts, such as pecans

NOTE This dough must be prepared in advance. Pecans are traditionally in these cookies in the United States, though any nut could be substituted. Want to change up the recipe? Try making them with macadamia nuts.

In a small bowl, whisk together the flour and salt, and reserve. In the bowl of an electric mixer on medium-high speed, beat the butter until creamy, about 1 minute. Reduce the speed to low, add ½ cup powdered sugar and vanilla extract, and mix until combined. Increase the speed to medium-high and beat until light and fluffy, about 2 minutes. Reduce the speed to low, add the flour mixture, and mix until just combined. Stir in the nuts. Cover the bowl with plastic wrap and refrigerate for 30 minutes.

When ready to bake, preheat the oven to 400°F and line the baking sheets with parchment paper.

Shape the dough into 1-inch balls, and place 1 inch apart on the prepared baking sheets (the cookies do not spread). Bake until set but not brown, 10 to 12 minutes. Remove the cookies from the oven and cool 5 minutes. While the cookies are still warm, carefully roll them in powdered sugar. Transfer the cookies to a wire rack to cool completely; then roll them in powdered sugar a second time.

In the Kitchen with Hedvig

RICK NELSON

SOME OF MY HAPPIEST and most enduring baking memories were created when my grandmother, Hedvig Nelson, would visit and devote a day—or several days—to baking up a storm in the cramped kitchen of my family's suburban Minneapolis home.

Decades later, Mom admitted that her mother-in-law's frequent bake-a-thons were stressful. From my perspective, Hedvig was a doting grandmother with mystical kitchen powers. To her daughter-in-law, Hedvig could be . . . challenging.

"If I bought Pillsbury flour, then she said I should have bought Gold Medal, and if I bought Gold Medal, then she said I should have bought Pillsbury," Mom recalled. "And on, and on, and on. But your grandmother was an extraordinary baker, and we all benefited from her generosity."

We sure did. In a blue gingham apron of her own design and making—which I still have, a treasured possession—Hedvig would diligently fill the ancient freezer in our garage with all kinds of goodies: golden cloverleaf dinner rolls, arched loaves of whole wheat sandwich bread, and pans of her famous caramel rolls, which are still talked about in my family with awe and affection fifty years later. Now that's a legacy.

Grandma, the daughter of Swedish immigrants, could seem to make something out of nothing, with a no-nonsense skill set sharpened by her impoverished childhood and the challenges of raising a large family during the Great Depression.

Under her watchful eye, nothing went to waste. She reused aluminum foil and plastic bags until they fell apart. Leftover mashed potatoes at dinner would become the building block of a loaf of her delicious potato bread the next morning. Extra cooked rice was patiently collected and frozen until enough was saved to create the rice pudding that my father adored.

Hedvig's considerable homemaking skills extended beyond the kitchen. She made beautiful clothes for my sisters and their dolls, cutting her own patterns and coaxing miracles out of an ancient Singer sewing machine. Her modest Robbinsdale apartment was always spotless. And because she grew up on a farm in Anoka County, Hedvig was a veteran gardener.

I loved watching her in bread-baking mode, with her well-practiced know-how on display. She was an instinctual baker, relying on her senses and spontaneity instead of the precision of measuring cups and kitchen scales. At the time, I was too young to recognize the importance of what I was witnessing. Today, I would capture some of the nuances behind her baking rituals with my iPhone, since she rarely committed her recipes to pen and paper.

The exception was cakes and cookies. Those instructions were recorded in culinary shorthand on small index cards that she'd pull out of her purse at our house.

Her cookies! She'd cover the kitchen table with a steady stream of delicate sugar cutouts, perfumed with almond extract and twinkling with bright decorative sugars. Grandma would transform Hills Bros. and McGarvey coffee cans into cookie jars, filling them with batches of chewy, nutmeg-scented, raisin-studded oatmeal cookies.

But what I craved most were her Ranger Cookies. Not that they were "hers." Because a primary ingredient is Wheaties, Hedvig probably found the recipe on the back of a cereal box. Or maybe she saw it in the then-ubiquitous *Betty Crocker's Cooky Book* (a Ranger Cookies facsimile, Cereal Coconut Cookies, is on page 67 of my late mother's well-worn copy). But I'm fairly certain that Grandma didn't own many cookbooks, let alone one that would have had the temerity to tell her how to bake.

My version of Ranger Cookies is based on my sister Linda's handwritten transcription of Grandma's recipe, probably from the early 1970s. Since then I've made a few alterations, including adding a decorative chocolate drizzle. I'm guessing that Hedvig would have rejected that idea as an unnecessary extravagance.

My affection for a cookie that gets its quiet crunch from the Breakfast of Champions runs counter to how I viewed entries during my 20-year involvement in the *Star Tribune* Holiday Cookie Contest. As we sorted through submissions, I rejected any that incorporated breakfast cereals; cookies, I argued, should be made with wholesome ingredients, not Cap'n Crunch, Froot Loops, or Count Chocula.

Do as I say, and not as I do? For these delicious cookies, guilty as charged.

Ranger Cookies

MAKES 3 DOZEN COOKIES

2 cups flour
1/4 teaspoon baking soda
1/4 teaspoon baking powder
1/2 teaspoon salt
1/4 teaspoon freshly grated nutmeg
1 cup (2 sticks) unsalted butter, at room temperature
1/2 cup granulated sugar
1/2 cup packed light brown sugar
2 eggs
1 teaspoon vanilla extract
1 cup rolled oats (see Note)
1 cup crushed Wheaties, Total, or other wheat flakes cereal
1/2 cup sweetened shredded coconut
4 ounces semisweet chocolate

NOTE For a more refined texture, place the rolled oats in a food processor fitted with a metal blade and pulse until the oats have an almond flour–like consistency.

Preheat the oven to 325°F and line the baking sheets with parchment paper. Place a wire rack over wax paper or parchment paper.

In a medium bowl, whisk together the flour, baking powder, baking soda, salt, and nutmeg, and reserve.

In the bowl of an electric mixer on medium-high speed, beat the butter until creamy, about 1 minute. Add the granulated sugar and brown sugar and beat until light and fluffy, about 2 minutes. Add the eggs, one at a time, and beat until thoroughly combined. Add the vanilla extract, and beat until thoroughly combined. Reduce the speed to low. Add the flour mixture in three additions, mixing until just combined. Stir in the rolled oats, crushed Wheaties (or other wheat flakes cereal), and the coconut.

Shape the dough into 1-inch balls, and place 2 inches apart on the prepared baking sheets. Bake until the cookies are lightly browned on the edges, about 9 to 11 minutes. Remove the cookies from the oven and cool for about 5 minutes before transferring them to the prepared wire rack to cool completely.

In a double boiler over gently simmering water (or in a bowl in a microwave oven), melt the chocolate, whisking occasionally until smooth. Drizzle the melted chocolate over the cookies. Allow the chocolate to set before serving.

Mrs. Hewitt's Molasses Crinkles

In a 2021 Taste story during back-to-school season, Rick declared this uncomplicated recipe the "ultimate lunchbox cookie." That's a big boast for a cookie that doesn't involve the words "chocolate chips," but the praise holds true. The recipe is based on a cookie that *Star Tribune* staff writer Chris Hewitt grew up eating. He shared his mother's recipe with Rick, who gradually fiddled with Judy Hewitt's formula, adding ingredients to boost the flavor but always preserving the cookie's crackled appearance and irresistibly tender-yet-chewy texture.

MAKES 3 DOZEN COOKIES

2 1/4 cups flour
1 teaspoon baking soda
1 1/2 teaspoons ground ginger
1/2 teaspoon ground cardamom
1/2 teaspoon ground cloves
1/4 teaspoon ground allspice
1/4 teaspoon freshly ground black pepper
1/4 teaspoon salt
3/4 cup (1 1/2 sticks) unsalted butter, at room temperature
1/2 cup plus 1/3 cup granulated sugar, plus extra for rolling dough
1/3 cup packed dark brown sugar
1 egg yolk
1 teaspoon vanilla extract
1/2 cup dark molasses

NOTE This dough must be prepared in advance.

In a medium bowl, whisk together the flour, baking soda, ginger, cardamom, cloves, allspice, black pepper, and salt, and reserve.

In the bowl of an electric mixer on medium-high speed, beat the butter until creamy, about 1 minute. Add the granulated sugar and brown sugar and beat until light and fluffy, about 2 minutes. Add the egg yolk and vanilla extract and beat until thoroughly combined.

Reduce the speed to low, add the molasses, and mix until thoroughly combined. Reduce the speed to low, add the flour mixture, and mix until just combined. Cover the bowl with plastic wrap and refrigerate at least 4 hours, or overnight.

When ready to bake, preheat the oven to 375°F and line the baking sheets with parchment paper.

Place about 1 cup granulated sugar into a shallow bowl. Shape the dough into 1-inch balls. Roll the cookies in the granulated sugar to coat and place 2 inches apart on the prepared baking sheets. Bake until the cookies are browned and slightly puffy, with cracks in the tops, about 11 minutes (if using a convection oven, check on them at 9 minutes: if the cookies are still slightly wet in the cracks, bake an additional 30 seconds). Remove the cookies from the oven and cool for about 5 minutes before transferring them to a wire rack to cool completely.

Chocolate Sugar Cookies

During the pandemic, these easy-to-prepare treats became a constant in Rick's baking repertoire. They're adapted from a recipe from *The Vanilla Bean Baking Book* by Minnesota cookbook author Sarah Kieffer. "The biggest thing with baking is patience, and practice," Kieffer said when Rick interviewed her for a 2020 Taste story. "You'll learn so much if you make a recipe over and over." Excellent advice, because this version of her recipe—which inserts brown sugar and instant espresso powder, bumps up the levels of cocoa powder and vanilla extract, and adds a refrigerated rest for the dough—is the happy result of repetition and experimentation.

MAKES 3 DOZEN COOKIES

1 3/4 cups flour

1/2 cup plus 2 tablespoons unsweetened cocoa powder

3/4 teaspoon baking soda

1/2 teaspoon instant espresso powder

1/2 teaspoon salt

1 cup (2 sticks) unsalted butter, at room temperature

1 1/4 cups granulated sugar, plus extra for rolling balls of dough

1/2 cup packed light brown sugar or dark brown sugar

1 egg

2 teaspoons vanilla extract

NOTE This dough must be prepared in advance.

In a medium bowl, whisk together the flour, cocoa powder, baking soda, espresso powder, and salt, and reserve.

In the bowl of an electric mixer on medium-high speed, beat the butter until creamy, about 1 minute. Add the granulated sugar and brown sugar and beat until light and fluffy, about 2 minutes. Add the egg and vanilla extract and beat until thoroughly combined. Reduce the speed to low, add the flour mixture, and mix until just combined. Cover the bowl with plastic wrap and refrigerate for at least 4 hours, or overnight.

When ready to bake, preheat the oven to 325°F and line the baking sheets with parchment paper. Place about 1 cup granulated sugar into a shallow bowl. Shape the dough into 1-inch balls. Roll the cookies in the granulated sugar to coat and place 2 inches apart on the prepared baking sheets. Bake until the cookies are slightly puffy, with cracks in the tops, about 9 to 11 minutes. Remove the cookies from the oven and cool for about 5 minutes before transferring them to a wire rack to cool completely.

Sesame Ginger Cookies with Miso

Starting in 2015, pastry chef and culinary instructor Amy Carter became an indispensable part of our contest, recruiting and leading a crew of pastry chefs to bake our semifinalist entries and then becoming one of our most discerning judges. Amy was visiting the cafe at Alma in Minneapolis when she developed an immediate obsession with pastry chef Jessica Vostinar's tahini-miso cookie. Amy was inspired to create a bake-at-home version, using a peanut butter cookie recipe as a foundation. Rather than making a drop cookie, she turned to the bar cookie format. "It's because they were doing cookies at Alma," she said. "I wanted to use those flavors, but I didn't want to just take their cookie." Rick, another devoted fan of Vostinar's imaginative and skilled handiwork, convinced (OK, it was more like *bugged*) Amy to make a cookie. After many trial runs, Amy landed on this easy-to-prepare recipe, which is an affectionate tribute to—but not a carbon copy of—Vostinar's umami-laced creation.

MAKES 3 DOZEN COOKIES

2 cups flour

4 tablespoons ground ginger, divided

1 1/2 teaspoons baking powder

1 teaspoon baking soda

1/2 cup sesame seeds, divided

1/2 cup (1 stick) unsalted butter, at room temperature

1 1/2 cups packed light brown sugar or dark brown sugar

1 cup tahini

1/4 cup white miso

2 eggs

1 cup granulated sugar

NOTE This dough must be prepared in advance.

In a medium bowl, whisk together the flour, 2 tablespoons ginger, baking powder, baking soda, and 1/4 cup of sesame seeds, and reserve.

In the bowl of an electric mixer on medium-high speed, beat the butter until creamy, about 1 minute. Add the brown sugar and beat until light and fluffy, about 2 minutes.

Add the tahini and white miso and beat until thoroughly combined. Add the eggs, one at a time, beating well after each addition. Reduce the speed to low, add the flour mixture, and mix until just combined. Cover the bowl with plastic wrap and refrigerate for at least 4 hours, or overnight.

When ready to bake, preheat the oven to 325°F and line the baking sheets with parchment paper.

In a shallow bowl, combine the remaining 2 tablespoons ground ginger and the remaining 1/4 cup sesame seeds with the granulated sugar. Shape the dough into 1-inch balls. Roll the cookies in the ginger-sesame seeds-granulated sugar mixture to coat and place 2 inches apart on the prepared baking sheets. Bake until the cookies are browned and slightly puffy, with cracks in the tops, about 11 to 12 minutes.

Remove the cookies from the oven and cool for about 5 minutes before transferring them to a wire rack to cool completely.

The Ultimate Cookie Pairing

RICK NELSON

WHEN I WAS GROWING UP, my father's extended family gathered on Christmas Eve for an enormous, controlled-pandemonium celebration. My dad or one of his brothers would gamely pull on an ill-fitting Santa suit (their wingtips always gave them up as sub-urban stand-ins for the real St. Nick), and my mom and aunts would prepare an enormous buffet potluck supper. Dessert was invariably lefse and cookies, and I quickly learned to gravitate toward the platter prepared by Aunt Marge Hermstad, a woman who definitely knew her way around flour, eggs, butter, and sugar.

We're talking about the late 1960s here, so forgive my cobwebbed memory, but I can recall ignoring julekake, toffee bars, date balls, and other goodies in favor of what my preadolescent brain decided was the cookie embodiment of the True Meaning of Christmas. In other words, Marge's Peanut Butter Blossoms.

Their allure? Simple. An entire Hershey's Kiss, a wildly extravagant culinary gesture.

The cookie, a tender, crackle-topped peanut butter treat, was a big draw too, par-ticularly since I practically lived on peanut butter (and, truth to tell, still do).

Now, all these years later, I continue to nurture a not-so-secret crush on the cookie also known as the Peanut Blossom, a Pillsbury Bake-Off finalist from 1957. I've always enjoyed baking them too. They come together in a snap, and they routinely elicit "Oh, my favorite," a phrase that bakers every-where never tire of hearing.

Through trial and error, I've discovered that the secret to Peanut Butter Blossom success is to forgo the Jif–Skippy universe in favor of an all-natural peanut butter. I don't even mind the tedious task of extricating all of those Kisses from their foil wrappers, probably because it's an unwritten require-ment that the cook sneak a few. Okay, more than a few.

I'll never forget when Aunt Marge, true to form, arrived for a summertime lunch on our screen porch with a generous gift from her kitchen: a plastic container filled with brownies. Treasure, truly. They were delicious. A few weeks later, trying to be the thought-ful nephew that she deserved, I returned her Tupperware to her, filling it with Peanut Butter Blossoms.

Peanut Butter Blossoms

MAKES 3 DOZEN COOKIES

1 ¼ cups flour
1 teaspoon baking soda
½ teaspoon salt
½ cup (1 stick) unsalted butter, at room
    temperature
1 cup creamy, unsalted, natural (not
    hydrogenated) peanut butter
½ cup granulated sugar, plus more for
    coating
½ cup packed light brown sugar
½ teaspoon vanilla extract
1 egg
36 milk chocolate kisses, unwrapped

NOTE This dough must be prepared in advance. Adapted from *A Baker's Field Guide to Christmas Cookies,* by Dede Wilson.

In a medium bowl, whisk together the flour, baking soda, and salt, and reserve.

In the bowl of an electric mixer on medium-high speed, beat the butter and peanut butter together until creamy, about 2 minutes. Add 1/2 cup granulated sugar and brown sugar, and beat until light and fluffy, about 2 minutes. Add the vanilla extract and egg, and mix until fully combined. Reduce the speed to low. Add one-third of the flour mixture and mix until just combined. Gradually add the remaining flour mixture, mixing until just combined.

Form the dough into a disk, wrap in plastic wrap, and refrigerate at least 1 hour, or overnight.

When ready to bake, preheat the oven to 350°F and line the baking sheets with parchment paper. Shape the dough into 1 1/2-inch balls. Roll the cookies in granulated sugar, coating them completely, and place 2 inches apart on the prepared baking sheets. Gently flatten the cookies just enough so they don't roll off the baking sheets. Bake just until light golden brown on the bottoms, about 12 to 14 minutes. Remove from the oven, gently press a chocolate kiss into the center of each cookie (cookies may crack; that's okay), and return the cookies to the oven for 1 minute. Remove the cookies from the oven and cool for 2 minutes before transferring them to a wire rack to cool completely.

Cookie…or Not?

TO BE OR NOT TO BE…A COOKIE

THAT IS THE QUESTION we were asked whenever a recipe for bars landed on the contest's finalist list. The discussion really heated up when the winning entry was a bar, as in 2009 for Almond Triangles and in 2020 for Spumoni Squares. Here's the logic behind our not-so-scientific definition.

LEE: We need an explanation of our cookie contest "rule" that allowed bars, those flat, soft squares prepared in a cake pan. What were you thinking?

RICK: Of course they're cookies, filed under B, for Bar Cookies. Some would even argue S, for Sheet Cookies, but I won't go that far.

LEE: Hmmm. If it looks like a bar, and tastes like a bar, how can it not be a bar?

RICK: I'm old enough to remember when Nestlé began promoting the concept of pressing Toll House cookie dough into a 9- by 13-inch pan. Same recipe, slightly different technique. How is that not a cookie? Rather, it's a "bar cookie."

LEE: You've got me there. If Toll House (perhaps the most famous cookie inspiration of all) thinks a cookie can be a bar, then we can consider the possibility that a bar is a cookie, though I would have a hard time rationalizing Rice Krispies bars as cookies.

RICK: Perhaps that's why Kellogg's calls them Rice Krispies *Treats*, to avoid the bar versus cookie conundrum. Since the chief ingredient is a breakfast cereal, and not flour, I'd say that Rice Krispies Treats are definitely not cookies, bar or otherwise. Most bars qualify as bar cookies, with the major exception of brownies. Brownies, and possibly their cousin, blondies, are always bars.

LEE: Define the sweet that most of us call a "cookie" and explain why a brownie—and a blondie—doesn't fit.

RICK: I'm going to channel Alton Brown, TV culinary host and author, and mention physics. Mix all brownie ingredients together, and a batter is formed. A pourable batter. But when cookie ingredients are mixed, they form a dough, one that (generally) holds its shape.

LEE: I wonder if Betty Crocker (aka General Mills) used the same logic when bars were included in her cookie book.

RICK: Ah, the famous *Betty Crocker's Cooky Book*, which was published by Minnesota-based General Mills and was a baking Bible in nearly every household in America in the 1960s and 1970s, mine included.

LEE: Mine, too. What about Nanaimo bars, the unbaked, three-layer bar from Canada's British Columbia that is well known in the Northwest? I don't remember anyone calling them "cookies" or even "bar cookies."

RICK: Remember when we published a no-bake recipe? That much-debated inclusion of Kit-Kat Treats in 2015 (another bar cookie!) may have stirred more internal controversy than any cookie-versus-bar cookie discussion in the contest.

LEE: Ah, yes. Can an unbaked goodie be part of a baking contest? Deep thoughts for the

kitchen. Who knew contests—and cookies—could fall into a philosophical rabbit hole? For years during the cookie contest, we ignored entries that were unbaked, but that Kit-Kat recipe was too tasty to exclude. Which raises the question: is there a term for a baker who prepares an unbaked treat? Still a baker, or a cook?

RICK: Good question. The Kit-Kat recipe involves a saucepan and a stove, so "cook"?

LEE: Batter versus dough . . . I surrender. That's the best argument I've heard, notwithstanding the written support of virtually all baking books, which regularly list bars under "bar cookies." Even the Rice Krispies and Nanaimo versions. Sigh. I think I need a cookie. You may need to talk with Betty and Martha, who consider brownies to be bars.

RICK: They do? This is the first time that either one has ever let me down.

Nanaimo Bars

MAKES 2 TO 3 DOZEN BARS

FOR BASE

1/2 cup (1 stick) unsalted butter

1/4 cup granulated sugar

5 tablespoons unsweetened cocoa powder

1 egg, slightly beaten

1 teaspoon vanilla extract

2 cups graham cracker crumbs (from about 32 square crackers)

1 cup sweetened shredded coconut

1/2 cup finely chopped almonds

FOR FILLING

1/4 cup (1/2 stick) unsalted butter, at room temperature

2 tablespoons custard powder or vanilla instant pudding mix

2 tablespoons heavy cream, plus extra if needed

2 cups powdered sugar

FOR GLAZE

4 ounces semisweet chocolate

2 tablespoons unsalted butter

NOTE This recipe (pronounced nuh-NI-mow), named for a Canadian city, must be prepared in advance. Custard powder is available in specialty stores and some supermarkets, as well as online. The powder gives the filling its requisite yellow color; vanilla instant pudding mix will create a similar result. Instead of almonds, try walnuts or pecans, or a mixture.

TO PREPARE BASE: In a medium saucepan over medium heat, melt the butter. Reduce the heat to medium-low and add the granulated sugar and cocoa powder, stirring until well combined. Add the egg and cook, stirring, until the mixture begins to thicken. Remove the pan from the heat and stir in the vanilla extract, cracker crumbs, coconut, and almonds. Press the mixture into a 9- by 9-inch baking pan.

TO PREPARE FILLING: In the bowl of an electric mixer, beat the butter and custard powder (or instant pudding mix) on medium speed until creamy, about 1 minute. Add the cream and beat until well combined. Reduce the speed to low and add the powdered sugar, one-half cup at a time, mixing until creamy, adjusting with more cream as needed, 1 teaspoon at a time. Spread the filling over the base layer. Refrigerate for at least 30 minutes.

TO PREPARE GLAZE: In a double boiler over gently simmering water (or in a bowl in a microwave oven), melt the semisweet chocolate, whisking occasionally until smooth. Remove from heat, add the butter, and whisk until the butter is melted and thoroughly combined. Allow the chocolate mixture to cool slightly, then spread it over the filling. Return the baking pan to the refrigerator for at least 1 hour. Cut into small bar cookies.

Acknowledgments

OUR SINCERE THANKS to the thousands of *Star Tribune* readers who enthusiastically shared their recipes and stories. Without them, we would not have had a contest. That collective involvement and interest—and, yes, excitement, exuberance, and creativity—made this book possible.

We're grateful for our *Star Tribune* colleagues (too numerous to mention here) who helped keep the cookie contest alive and thriving for twenty years, including the dozens who pitched in to bake and assess our semifinalist recipes. A special shout-out to Meredith Deeds, Nicole Hvidsten, Sharyn Jackson, and Kim Ode.

A big thank you to Amy Carter and Matt Deutsch for their baking expertise and generosity, and to their students and former students from Art Institutes International Minnesota and Burnsville High School for their significant contributions to our semifinalist judging process.

Thanks to the *Star Tribune* leadership for supporting our Holiday Cookie Contest. No one flinched when we said, "Let's hold a recipe competition." Not once in twenty years.

We appreciate the work of food stylists Carmen Bonilla and Lisa Golden Schroeder, who prepared many of the cookies for photography (we baked the less-than-perfect ones).

A heartfelt thanks to the University of Minnesota Press for bringing these recipes to a wider audience. We're especially grateful to our discerning editor Erik Anderson, who knew a winning recipe when he saw one.

And thanks to all of those who love cookies! What could be a better treat? Bring on the flour, sugar, butter, and eggs. We have some baking to do.

We also have personal thanks to offer for our cookie-making skills:

LEE SVITAK DEAN: The cookie jar always overflowed in the Svitak kitchen, thanks to my mother, Laverne, who kept us with a ready supply of sugar cookies, gingersnaps, and more. So many more. I never had a commercially made sweet until, on a rare occasion, my earnest request was fulfilled (please, please, an Oreo, Mallomar, or sugar wafer so I could be like every other classmate with a packaged treat in her lunchbox). My mother's sisters, Joan Odden and Clarice Granz, were equally prolific bakers, with ready supplies of their favorites offered to any visitor. When the Christmas holidays arrived, they all went crazy with cookies, especially the Norwegian treats, including sandbakkels, krumkake, and rosettes, with the guidance of my grandmother Martha Nelson. On separate occasions, she patiently supervised the baking and frosting of cutout cookies with her grandchildren. I do the same with my three grands today, cleaning up sprinkles for weeks. From those family bakers, I've learned the secret to making every day better: eat a cookie. It's as simple as that. And, from my colleagues Rick and Tom, I've learned that nothing is sweeter than a collaboration with friends.

RICK NELSON: I was fortunate to grow up in a loving family of cookie enthusiasts, including grandmothers Gay Olsen and

Hedvig Nelson, great-aunts Alice Moe and Marian Moe, and aunts Patricia Hoyt, Carolyn Brunelle, Mary Olsen, Susan Nyhammer, Susan Olsen, Millie Carlson, Marge Hermstad, Elzina Nelson, Jan Nelson, and Norrie Nelson.

I'm forever grateful for my wonderful mother, Judy Nelson, who instilled an everlasting love of Christmas—and Christmas cookies—in me and my siblings: Cheri Trench, Todd Nelson, and ace cookie baker Linda Korman. Thanks to my husband, Robert Davidian, for his support and for having the instinct to take only the ugly cookies off the test-batch tray.

My cookie-baking role models extend to an impressive and inspiring group of Minnesota (and Wisconsin) pastry chefs, bakers, and bakery owners. Writing about them and their work was one of the highlights of my twenty-four years at the *Star Tribune*. I have nothing but admiration for Soile Anderson, Anne Andrus, Sarah Botcher, Katie Elsing, Zoë François, Michelle Gayer, Lynn Gordon, Marc Heu, Steve Horton, Peter Kelsey, Sarah Kieffer, François Kiemde, John Kraus, Brett Laidlaw, Michael Lillegard, Laurie Lin, Erin Lucas, Emily Marks, Shawn McKenzie, Diane Moua, Susan Muskat, Ruth Raich, Annamarie Rigelman, Anne Rucker, Patti Soskin, Carrie Summer, Sandra Thielman, Solveig Tofte, and Mala Vujnovich.

Finally, thanks to my co-conspirators Lee and Tom, for this book and its 2018 predecessor, and for many happy years of collaboration in the *Star Tribune* newsroom. I loved making Taste with you.

TOM WALLACE: I'd like to acknowledge all of the people who are inspired by a contest. Their creativity, energy, and sense of fun have been the driving forces behind this treasured Minnesota tradition.

Thanks to Steve Rice, former *Star Tribune* director of photography, and Rhonda Prast, former art director for the *Star Tribune* Taste section, for being all-in on the contest and for supporting my work. Thanks also to former *Star Tribune* photographer Stormi Greener, for being a partner in crime during the contest's early years and for pushing me to try to do my best work.

There aren't a lot of people who would deal with an annual project like the cookie contest, because it's no easy task. But Lee and Rick did and, when I look back at what we did during those twenty years, it's a pretty cool piece of community journalism. Together, we developed something special.

I also acknowledge my wife, Regina Marie Williams, for putting up with me, especially when I took over her garage to shoot a bunch of cookies.

Indexes

Cookies A–Z

Cookies by Category

CHOCOLATE

EASY

Cookies by Contest Year

Contest Bakers

LEE SVITAK DEAN wrote about food for four decades at the *Star Tribune*, twenty-six of those years as editor of the Taste section, where she guided its food coverage to multiple James Beard Awards as well as an Emmy and national recognition as "Best Food Section." She is the author of *Come One, Come All: Easy Entertaining with Seasonal Menus.*

RICK NELSON was the *Star Tribune*'s restaurant critic and food writer for twenty-four years. He is a James Beard Award winner, and his writing has been published in four editions of the annual *Best Food Writing* anthologies, which present the best of American food journalism.

TOM WALLACE had a long, award-winning career in small-town community journalism before he arrived at the *Star Tribune* as a photographer and photo editor. He used those skills to showcase food at its best for the newspaper's Taste section and received national recognition for his work.